D1067507

Guerrilla

Books by Charles W. Thayer

Nonfiction

GUERRILLA

DIPLOMAT

THE UNQUIET GERMANS

BEARS IN THE CAVIAR

HANDS ACROSS THE CAVIAR

RUSSIA (*with the editors of* Life)

Fiction

MOSCOW INTERLUDE

Guerrilla

By CHARLES W. THAYER

Foreword by Sir Fitzroy Maclean

69242

HARPER & ROW, PUBLISHERS

NEW YORK, EVANSTON, AND LONDON

LIBRARY OF CONGRESS CATALOG CARD NUMBER: 63-16521

A-R

To

W. P. Y.

and the men of the U.S. Army Special Forces

Contents

viii)   CONTENTS

Acknowledgments

Many more people than I could list here have helped me in the preparation of this volume. However, I should like to record my special thanks to the following persons who have read and criticized portions of the manuscript:

W. Averell Harriman, Deputy Under Secretary of State, Department of State; James Eliot Cross, himself an expert on the subject and author of *Conflict in the Shadows*; Samuel B. Griffith, Brigadier General, USMC, ret., whose scholarly and graceful translations of Mao Tse-tung and Sung Tzu I have quoted extensively.

Roger Hilsman, a former practitioner of the art and at the time of writing Director of Intelligence and Research, Department of State; Victor H. Krulak, Major General, USMC, Special Assistant for Counter Insurgency and Special Activities, Joint Chiefs of Staff; Edward G. Lansdale, Major General, USAF, who supplied much of the material on Magsaysay's campaign against the x)   ACKNOWLEDGMENTS

Huks; Tad Szulc of the *New York Times* and co-author of *The Cuban Invasion* from which I have drawn much of my material on the subject; Chalmers B. Wood, Officer in Charge of Vietnam Affairs, Department of State.

I am especially indebted to my fellow cadet at West Point, Major General William P. Yarborough, Commander of the U.S. Army Special Warfare School, and the members of his staff both for helping me plan this volume and for checking the finished manuscript.

Finally I should like to thank Rogelio David of Washington, D.C., for his careful and thorough research for this study.

As will be readily apparent, the opinions of those named above do not always correspond with my own.

C. W. T.

Foreword

Mr. Thayer's book comes at one of those periods in history when, as a by-product of the Cold War, irregular warfare is in the news. It is a subject on which he writes with authority, having had wide firsthand experience of Communists and Communism and having, in particular, served during the war with Tito's Partisans, a useful forcing ground for irregular soldiers. Moreover, despite his West Point training and his distinguished services as a career diplomat, he possesses, among other attributes, the sort of mind which makes a man a natural guerrilla. It was my knowledge of this fact, coupled with a predilection for his entertaining company, which caused me in 1944 to use such influence as I had with him and with the Allied High Command to encourage his transfer to the Yugoslav theater of operations.

The publication, nearly twenty years later, of his present work is greatly to be welcomed. It throws a penetrating and badly needed light on a problem of great topicality and importance.

Much was achieved by the irregular forces of the Allies in the last war. Much more could have been achieved if more thought had been given to this subject in advance. The same considerations apply even more forcibly today.

So long as the present ideological conflict between East and West continues, so long as the mutual balance of terror makes a hot war improbable, and so long as the stresses and strains of nationalism and racialism add fuel to the fire, the Western Allies are likely to find themselves involved willy-nilly in a prolonged series of cold war operations, in many of which, by their very nature, the guerrilla and the counter-guerrilla will inevitably have their part to play. It is therefore important to keep under constant review the laws and principles which govern the conduct of irregular warfare.

Because they spring from the very nature of guerrilla warfare, these principles possess a certain stability. The first, as it has always been, remains mobility and a capacity for taking the enemy by surprise, what Lawrence called "the irrational tenth, like the kingfisher flashing across a pool." Guerrilla warfare is a war of movement in its extreme form. It also needs to be a war in depth. Because the guerrilla is almost always outgunned and outnumbered, he needs a background, a hinterland from which and in which he can operate, and into which he can fade back when things become too difficult for him. Forests or mountains or desert, even the tenements and sewers of a great city.

Against this background the guerrilla must be what Lawrence called "an idea, a thing invulnerable, intangible, without front or back, drifting about like a gas." He must be on the move the whole time, so as not to present a target at which the enemy can strike back. His must be a war of detachment; he must at all costs avoid a war of contact, of pitched battles against tanks and aircraft. To become involved in such a battle is a thing which in my own experience of irregular war has happened to me two or three times and which I would much sooner did not happen to me again.

"An ability to run away," according to Mao Tse-tung, "is the great characteristic of the guerrilla." On the other hand, while the guerrilla is likely from his very nature to be strategically on the defensive, it is vital that whenever possible he should be tactically on the offensive; that, when threatened with a pitched battle, he should extricate himself, but immediately afterward hit the enemy again as hard as he can where it hurts most.

To make such resilience and endurance possible, leadership, discipline (which in practice means self-discipline), and morale are of the highest importance. To achieve these the guerrilla must be fortified and inspired by a strong idea, patriotic, religious, political, or a mixture of all three. "We had won a province," wrote Lawrence, "when we had taught the civilians in it to die for our idea of freedom." And Napoleon writing of Spain, where the very word guerrilla has its origin, said that moral considerations made up three-quarters of the game and the relative balance of military power accounted only for the remaining quarter. Finally, and the two principles go hand in hand, to subsist at all, the guerrilla must be close to the local population. He must, in the words of Mao Tse-tung's famous maxim, live among the people as the fish lives in the water.

No less important than the guerrilla in these troubled times is the counter-guerrilla. "To make war on rebellion," it has been said, "is messy and slow, like eating soup with a knife." Some hold that you must fight guerrillas with regular troops; others that against guerrillas you must use guerrillas of your own. The answer probably lies somewhere between the two. A good general rule is to take the basic principles of guerrilla warfare and apply them in reverse. The guerrilla's first principle being mobility, your first object, if you are fighting against guerrillas, must be to deny them mobility, to pin them down, and encircle them. Again you must try to deny them the element of surprise; in fact you must use it against them. Equally, while they try to avoid a pitched battle, you must try to force them into a pitched battle. They need the support of the local population. You must at all costs deny it them. Finally, against their strong idea, you must set a stronger idea that in the long run will prevail and win.

In *Guerrilla,* which, in addition to some highly pertinent flash-backs, covers pretty well the whole range of irregular operations during the postwar years, Mr. Thayer illustrates these and many other principles by a number of graphic examples, skillfully chosen from the irregular campaigns of the last twenty years. It is to be hoped that those in our respective countries who are concerned with such matters will study these examples and the valuable conclusions which he draws from them with the attention that they deserve. Only thus can they be prevented, as he so elegantly puts it, from continuing to wallow in successive Bays of Pigs.

FITZROY MACLEAN

Introduction

How ill-armed, ill-trained and ill-clad bands led by amateur soldiers so frequently succeed against superior forces led by professionals is the subject of this volume. It is not addressed primarily to the specialists—to those concerned with the technical and tactical problems of guerrilla operations. It does not profess to tell how to lay an ambush or to avoid getting caught in one, how to blow up a culvert or climb into a tree or out of one if your parachute gets hung up in it. Library shelves groan under the weight of treatises dealing more than adequately with these questions.

On the other hand, it does attempt to probe deeper into the basic causes of guerrilla conflicts, the sources of their amazing power and their hidden weaknesses. And finally it suggests ways by which such movements can be forestalled and their vulnerabilities exploited.

Among many professional as well as amateur soldiers there is a widespread and complacent misconception that guerillas are romantic vestiges of the past or confined to remote exotic jungles beyond the periphery of our national defenses. While it is true that guerillas are as old as history, in the years since World War II they have become the predominant form of armed conflict throughout the world. In China, Yugoslavia, Indochina and Cuba they have achieved their goals. In Greece, Malaya and the Philippines they have come within a hair's breadth of overthrowing our friends and allies. In Algeria and Indonesia they have fought their enemies to a standstill. In Cyprus and Kenya guerrillas have been defeated only by costly military efforts combined with far-reaching political concessions.

Today, on every continent conditions prevail that resolute guerrillas, Communist and non-Communist, may at any time try to exploit and thus confront us with a challenge to defend our friends against Communist dictatorships of the Left or authoritarian dictatorships of the Right. Nor can we overlook the possibility that we may be called upon to support active guerrilla movements against despotic regimes. It is therefore essential to develop our capacity not only to defend our friends in counterinsurgent operations but also to support them in guerrilla operations against tyrants in power.

Guerrilla warfare has been defined as "an irregular war carried on by independent bands." It can be divided into two types according to the circumstances of its origin. It may be a spontaneous uprising of part of the population against its own government, in which case it is a rebellion and may, if it grows, develop into a revolution. The early stages of the American Revolution and Castro's revolution against Batista would be examples of this type. Though both derived some support from outside, they were predominantly native uprisings which eventually developed into full-scale revolutions. In the American Revolution the scattered bands quickly consolidated into a conventional army and carried on regular warfare. In Castro's case, the government of Batista collapsed before the guerrillas consolidated. The Mau Mau uprising and the Algerian revolution also fall under this heading.

In the second case, the uprising is either instigated by or derives its chief support from a neighboring country attempting to weaken, harass or overthrow its enemy indirectly by exploiting discontented elements in the enemy's own country or in countries occupied by the enemy's forces. In this case it is often called "resistance." Julian Amery, an ex-practitioner of the art, defines resistance as "operations directed against an enemy behind his lines by discontented elements among the enemy or enemy-occupied population." The enemy may be a conventional belligerent, an enemy in cold war, a malevolent neutral or any state against which resistance is conducted. According to Amery, resistance can take the form of revolt, sabotage, guerrilla bands, terror or civil disobedience, spreading propaganda or harboring agents and escaped prisoners. During World War II, the Maquis in France, both Tito and Mikhailovitch in Yugoslavia and the anti-Japanese guerrillas in Southeast Asia were resistance movements. Today Communist-inspired "liberation wars" fall under this heading.

For the purposes of the present study, the term guerrilla warfare covers both types except that it would exclude mere passive resistance and subversive propaganda campaigns unaccompanied by the use of force. Guerrilla warfare can develop into conventional warfare when it possesses sufficient forces and equipment to challenge a major enemy force in open combat. Or it can remain a guerrilla force operating as an auxiliary to organized armies behind enemy lines—or it can be wiped out.

The classical studies of the art of war, including Clausewitz, have heretofore paid little attention to the theory or philosophy of unconvential war. In fact many generals even today harbor a deep-seated aversion to guerrillas, apparently because they fit no conventional pattern and their underhanded, clandestine tactics have little in common with the military code of honor and chivalry which career soldiers even in the age of carpet bombing like to associate with their profession.

However, even Clausewitz, the Prussian, points out that "Each age has had its own peculiar forms of war, its own restrictive conditions and its own prejudices." While he does not foresee the restrictive conditions imposed by nuclear weapons, he does emphasize the growing role of the masses of the population in war since the French Revolution. In his brief but penetrating account of the development of modern war, he stops just short of predicting the popular movements which have become one of the peculiar forms of war in an age that followed his by a hundred years. Clausewitz traces the art of war from the Tartar invasions down to the Napoleonic period. The Tartar hordes, he points out, were largely composed of warriors together with their families. Their objective was generally fresh pasture land or loot. Their method was to annihilate or simply drive off the occupants of lands they desired. They were in fact a nation under arms. "The people," Clausewitz says of the Tartars, "were everything in war."

In the old republics, with the exception of Rome, the armies were composed of only the privileged citizenry and as a result they were small and inconsequential, devoting their efforts largely to devastating the enemy's countryside and holding a town or two in hostage.

During the Middle Ages armies were for the most part composed of feudal levies, and war itself was confined to short periods of time. The soldiery was bound to its feudal lords partly by legal obligation, partly by voluntary contract. Single combat was common and war on a large scale unusual. "At no period," Clausewitz says, "has the union of states been so weak and the individual so independent."

From this system, however, the standing army was gradually developed. States became territorially more consolidated, and the mercenary the permanent employee of the state. As the states grew fewer in number and larger in extent, and as their internal unity under hereditary rulers increased, so did the standing army. Under Louis XIV the standing army reached its zenith. The military force was based on enlistment and pay. The pay derived from the state treasury, which the sovereign looked upon as his personal property. The relations between states too concerned not the people but the sovereigns. Thus the people, who in the Tartar invasions had been "everything," became in the eighteenth century "absolutely nothing" so far as war was concerned.

But then came the French Revolution and in its wake Napoleon Bonaparte. Now war suddenly again became an affair of the people. The whole weight of the nation, Clausewitz wrote, came into the scale. To defend themselves from the French, other nations had to follow suit and national armies began to be counted not in hundreds but in hundreds of thousands.

It was at this stage of the development of war that Clausewitz wrote his treatise, and he speculated briefly on whether future wars in Europe would be carried on with the whole power of the state or whether the interests of the government and the people would again diverge and armies again become the small, mercenary forces of the eighteenth century. Clausewitz tended to doubt it. Limits once broken, he indicated, are seldom re-established.

Clausewitz could not know, of course, that within a hundred years the limits would be extended far beyond anything even Napoleon had dreamed of. War would encompass not only the nation's adult male population but its entire industry and every resource. The bomber would bring war into homes far behind the front lines. Every woman and child would be made to feel its force. Though individuals or parties might control the destiny of the nation, every citizen would be obliged to fight for its defense either on the battlefield or in the factory.

With the development of the nuclear weapon and the rocket, war seems to have reached its ultimate limits. Its cost not only in money and resources but in casualties has made it all but prohibitive. Furthermore, the polarization of power between East and West has largely eliminated those potential combinations of force the manipulation of which provided one of the charms of war for statesmen a century ago.

Were the human race as basically peaceable as we would like to believe, we might be tempted to conclude that the prohibitive costs and equally prohibitive risks nuclear war entails had priced war itself out of the market. Unfortunately, there is too much evidence that the killing habit is deeply ingrained in human nature and that if one form of killing—the conventional war—is outlawed by the threat of nuclear suicide, man will find another less risky alternative.

This is especially true if the rivalries are over goals not achievable by conventional means. In the Middle Ages, rivals fought for towns or villages. In Napoleon's day they fought for whole nations. But today, as the level of mass education has risen, states tend to fight more and more for ideological goals. The ideologies themselves may be primitive as was Hitler's or demonstrably false as is the Kremlin's. But today whatever the personal ambitions of a national leader may be, he cannot hope to rally his people in an all-out war effort by appeals for conquest alone. His aim must be clothed in such slogans as *"lebensraum,"* "defense of democracy," "defense of Socialism," "liberation" or "self-determination."

Always resourceful, the militant Communist leaders faced with the dilemma of nuclear suicide or stagnation have delved back into history and come up with a form of conflict that, renovated and modernized, seems well suited to their needs. It is cheap in manpower and equipment, and allows its backers to employ native inhabitants of backward areas rather than their own troops.

Its instigation and support can up to a point be carried out clandestinely and in the event of failure can be disavowed. Its one drawback is that it must depend for its success on the blunders of the enemy.

It is important to remember, however, that guerrilla warfare was not invented by the Communists. The first guerrilla war on record was fought in China two thousand years before Marx. The Communists merely adopted and adapted it because it fitted so well into their theory of mass revolutions. In the first successful Communist revolution, the Russian guerrillas played a very small part and most of the fighting between the Red Army and its opponents was along conventional lines. Lenin and Stalin both predicted that when the revolutionary armies swept over the world, they would be aided by proletarian guerrilla bands fighting in the capitalists' rear against their own armies. Nothing of the sort has ever occurred. The Partisan armies fighting the Germans were Russians fighting not for revolution but for Mother Russia. The Polish and Yugoslav guerrillas fought for national independence, though in the latter case the movement was captured by Marxists and eventually diverted to the establishment of a Communist regime.

The first modern theorist of guerrilla warfare was not a Communist but a British scholar, T. E. Lawrence, who in his *Seven Pillars of Wisdom* outlined most of the basic strategic principles of unconventional war.

Nevertheless, the master-strategist of Communist guerrilla war, Mao Tse-tung, must be given credit for the first detailed study of unconventional warfare, its strategy and tactics. His writings provide the starting point for any study of modern guerrilla war. In subsequent chapters the basic principles he enunciates will be examined in greater detail. At this point only one of these principles concerns us, namely Mao's assertion that since guerrillas depend for their support on the population, counterrevolutionaries (i.e., non-Communists) cannot successfully fight guerrilla wars.

Communist doctrine aimed at rousing the masses to militant action against non-Communist systems is, of course, ideally suited to inspiring guerrilla bands against superior forces. However, it is by no means the only such appeal. One need go no further than the 1956 uprising in Budapest for proof that anti-Communist slogans can be equally effective in arousing the populace to heroic action against overwhelming odds.

Nor is Communist guerrilla warfare invariably successful. In 1948 the Kremlin called for uprisings in Burma, Malaya, Indonesia and Greece. All the movements were put down (though Burma and Indonesia are by no means "cleansed" of Communist influence).

Thus, guerrilla warfare is neither an invention nor a monopoly nor an invincible weapon of Communism. It is, rather, a particular form of warfare peculiarly suited to the restrictive conditions and prejudices of the present age.

Despite its peculiarities it is founded on many of the same principles that Clausewitz propounded for other forms of warfare. Probably the most famous of these principles is Clausewitz' statement that "war is nothing but a continuation of political intercourse, with a mixture of other means." The full implications of this statement will become clearer as we examine some of the peculiarities of guerrilla warfare in the subsequent chapters, and we shall return to this point in our conclusions.

Clausewitz also maintains that the effort to defeat an enemy is the product of two factors: the sum of available means, including the strength of the troops and their arms and equipment, plus the strength of will of the nation. Since almost by definition the means available to guerrillas are strictly limited, it follows that the strength of will of the guerrillas themselves and of their leaders must be of a high order.

Clausewitz also points out that in any war the sacrifice demanded of the enemy determines the extent of his resistance. If the demands of the guerrillas are moderate, their enemy is more likely to make peace—and vice versa.

The ultimate object of every war, says Clausewitz, is the political aim for which it was undertaken; the means to the end is the destruction of the enemy. However, he points out, victory does not always demand the destruction of the enemy's army— especially if he is stronger. In this case the means can be to raise the expenditure of strength by the enemy to the point where the price of success is too high. By far the most important way of accomplishing this is by wearing him out—a gradual exhaustion of his physical powers and of his will by long exertion. In the chapters that follow we shall see that the wearing out process and the exhaustion of the enemy's will are perhaps the most decisive strategy in guerrilla wars.

On the other hand, when one's own force is superior to the enemy's his defeat can be more promptly accomplished. In some wars it is only necessary to capture a province. In others it is essential to take the capital city. In still others, the physical destruction of the enemy is the sine qua non—as Napoleon learned in his Russian campaign where, by failing to destroy the army though he had captured a large section of the country and occupied Moscow, he was still defeated.

In such cases, Clausewitz warns, the commander must recognize where the center of gravity lies and direct the decisive effort against it. In states torn by internal dissensions it generally lies in the capital; in small states dependent on greater ones it usually lies in the army of these allies. (To have liberated Hungary in 1956, Washington realized that it would first have had to destroy the Soviet Army.) "In a national insurrection," Clausewitz concludes, "the center of gravity to be destroyed lies in the person of the chief leader and in public opinion; against these points the blow must be directed." In other words, he suggests that the heart of a guerrilla movement lies in its leadership and its mass appeal.

In the chapters that follow we shall examine in detail these twin hearts of a guerrilla movement—the character of its leadership and the cause for which it fights, as well as some of the other peculiarities and requirements of unconventional warfare which distinguish it from more familiar forms; and we shall analyze its capabilities and vulnerabilities.

But first, let us take a look at the way we have sought solutions in the immediate past to the challenge of unconventional war— in Vietnam to counter an insurgent operation and in Cuba to mount one.

1 As Prescribed by Regulations

GUERRILLAS never win wars but their adversaries often lose them.

Colonel Thanh of the South Vietnam Army was no exception. Commanding a 900-man regiment at Tayninh, about fifty miles due west of Saigon, Colonel Thanh had orders to hold down and if the opportunity offered to attack Communist Vietcong guerrilla forces operating in the area. He was a professionally trained soldier having participated in the training program drawn up by the United States Army M.A.A.G. group,* which had been active ever since 1954. He had obviously proved his competence or he would not have been given such a key job in so active an area.

The time was January 1960—the Vietnamese New Year's or *Tet* celebration. Because of the critical situation caused by repeated Vietcong attacks, President Diem himself had ordered that there would be no Tet celebrations in army camps and no holiday leaves for the soldiers. To the Vietnamese soldier Tet was comparable to a GI's Christmas and the order was an unpopular

* Military Aid and Advisory Group.

one. Some of Thanh's troops had grumbled angrily at this unreasonable restriction to quarters.

The cantonment itself was well guarded according to regulations. The jungle all around the headquarters huts, barracks, communications buildings and weapons stores had been cleared away. A series of towers at hundred-yard intervals had been erected around the perimeter and between them barbed wire had been strung. Furthermore, the troops had been drilled in repelling surprise attacks and each unit knew which section of the perimeter it must defend in case of alarm.

The day before, Colonel Thanh's intelligence officers had heard rumors through the grapevine that Vietcong guerrillas were contemplating an attack on his camp. Alert, he had sent out several patrols of thirty men each to sweep the surrounding forests. These troops had also been trained according to United States army manuals and had "swept" the mangrove jungles as thoroughly as the swampy area, the numerous canals and rivers permitted. But they had found no sign of any guerrillas. Colonel Thanh had reasonably enough concluded that the rumors were part of the war of nerves the Vietcong were constantly waging and had retired to his mud-walled, thatch-roofed quarters for a lonely but well-earned rest. When a few of his troops had slipped out of camp to attend some Tet celebrations in a neighboring village, his subordinates saw no reason to disturb his sleep (or interrupt his dreams, doubtless of celebrations with his family back in Saigon.)

Scarcely a mile from Thanh's headquarters, another Vietnamese, whom we can call Vinh Ho, smiled nervously when scouts reported a number of Thanh's troops celebrating in the village. It was just what he had hoped for. For weeks he had been planning for that night's operations. Time after time he had trained his guerrillas for the raid and had even set up a sand-table replica of Thanh's camp with which his chief subordinates had rehearsed every stage of the operation. In fact, his preparations had been almost too thorough, for evidently news of it had leaked to Thanh. Why else had he sent out those patrols the day before? Not that Vinh Ho was afraid of these conventional "sweeps." His guerrillas had long since learned to fade away into the underbrush when the Vietnamese regulars, weighed down with heavy weapons, knapsacks and equipment, crashed through the underbrush searching for them. Now as he waited for the moon to go down, messengers reported that his black-clad guerrillas, 300 strong, had sneaked into their prescribed positions around the perimeter. Behind them were another 300 men especially assembled for the purpose. These were not part of the fighting unit but peasants from nearby villages who, according to the Vietcong, had volunteered as auxiliaries and, according to Diem back in Saigon, had been impressed as porters. Slowly, silently, Vinh Ho crept toward the perimeter.

As he slipped forward a guerrilla, thoroughly rehearsed, crept through the barbed wire. It was not very difficult, for the guard posts were so far apart that without proper lights it was impossible for the sentries to observe the entire perimeter. Quietly he slid across the camp ground to Colonel Thanh's hut, slapped a handful of plastic explosive to the thick mud wall, lit a fuse and slipped back.

The first indication of the presence of Vinh's guerrillas and the signal for the general attack was when the wall of Colonel Thanh's hut dissolved in a blinding flash. Though the Colonel miraculously lived to face court martial, the explosion effectively knocked him out of further action. A moment later a squad of Vietcong charged each of the guard posts and quickly overpowered them. Another demolition group rushed the communications hut and with a few well-thrown grenades put the radio transmitter out of action.

As the Vietnamese troops dashed from their bunks to their assigned posts on the perimeter they discovered it was already overrun. While they milled about helplessly, another squad of Vietcong rushed the weapons room, and loaded its contents into the Vietnamese's own trucks, which they drove off down the jungle road to a rendezvous with the auxiliaries, who carried them off into the jungle.

When hours later a rescue column summoned by foot messengers finally arrived at Tayninh all they found were several score dead Vietnamese regulars and four or five guerrilla casualties. Back in the jungle Vinh Ho had 600 brand new American rifles—enough to arm a force twice as large as the one that had carried out the raid.

Today in South Vietnam over 10,000 American soldiers are engaged in a bitter jungle war which is costing the United States half a billion dollars a year and the outcome is by no means certain. The origins of the Vietnamese conflict and the American involvement in it during its early stages demonstrated all too clearly our failure to understand the fundamentals of this type of warfare and our inability to cope with it.

On July 20, 1954, the French gave up their struggle with the Communist forces in French Indochina and withdrew from their cherished overseas colony. Inevitably, the United States was drawn in to fill the vacuum left by the French and assumed the role of protector of the new Republic of South Vietnam under its President Diem. From 1954 until about 1959 Diem's regime showed a spectacular capacity for survival against enormous odds. Such guerrillas as were infiltrated from the Communist north confined themselves largely to terrorist assassinations of provincial and village leaders who supported Diem.

In 1957, the South Vietnamese government announced that "the Vietminh (North Vietnamese Communist) authorities have disintegrated and have been rendered powerless" in South Vietnam. Two years later a senior United States military adviser in Saigon reported to Washington that the Vietcong (Communist guerrillas) "were gradually nibbled away until they ceased to be a major menace to the country."*

* Quoted from Bernard B. Fall's *Street Without Joy*, Stackpole, Harrisburg, Pa.

Thus self-assured, the American military advisers set about organizing and training a South Vietnamese army in the only method of fighting with which the senior American generals in charge were familiar—the conventional European battles of World War II. The forces were grouped into conventional battalions and then into divisions, fully equipped with heavy artillery, tanks, motorized infantry and all the modern hardware of war. They even established two army corps with their cumbersome headquarters, and a third was planned.

While the military were thus engaged, American economic advisers were, with unassailable conventional logic, laying the foundations for the modernization of the country, beginning with such fundamental projects as rail, road and canal reconstruction and the building of basic industries in the larger towns, whence, it was hoped, industrial development would in time filter down to the villages. Similarly, the propaganda and educational facilities of the American mission in the South Vietnamese capital of Saigon were directed to laying the foundations for a sound democratic system of the conventional Western pattern, complete with government and loyal opposition. To this end every effort was made to win the minds of Saigon's intellectuals with symphony orchestras, art exhibits and similar cultural activities.

Had the Communist Vietminh in the north subscribed to convention, these efforts might well have succeeded. Unfortunately, however, the Communists persisted in playing by another set of rules. At first, it seems, they themselves had misjudged conditions in South Vietnam and after the French withdrawal had expected the weak, newborn regime of Diem to fall into their laps without any more effort than the occasional murder of one of Diem's supporters in the countryside. But even when the terrorists had accelerated their killings to as many as twenty-five a month by 1958, the Saigon government managed to prosper, partly as a result of Diem's vigor and partly as a result of massive American economic help.

Eventually, when the Vietminh realized that more energetic action was needed if Diem's regime was to be brought down, the terrorist campaign was transformed into a full-scale guerrilla operation.

Once again the Vietnamese and their American advisers reacted with predictable conventionality. Whenever a band of Vietcong guerrillas was located, Vietnamese regulars clattered after them in their tanks and found nothing. Time and again, the guerrillas slipped off into the jungle while the regular forces, roadbound by their heavy equipment, thrashed about the countryside in vain pursuit.

While the larger provincial towns were garrisoned, the small villages and hamlets were left to the guerrillas' mercies. Within a very short time, the villagers, whose need for economic assistance in the early years and for elementary defense in later years had been ignored by Saigon, swung their support to the guerrillas—or at best tried to stay neutral.

By 1960 large areas to within a few miles of Saigon itself were dominated by the guerrillas and Diem's writ ran only in the larger towns. Early that year a Vietcong force was strong enough to attack an entire battalion of Vietnamese regulars and make off with all its equipment.*

By 1961 for every guerrilla weapon captured by South Vietnamese troops, the guerrillas captured two from the regulars. The entire economy of the country was paralyzed and in that year Vietnam, normally a major exporter of rice, had to import 40,000 tons to feed the urban areas under its control.

As early as 1960, American political representatives in Saigon had begun to suspect that something was radically wrong with South Vietnamese strategy. With the help of Diem's supporters they drew up a plan for an entirely new approach and after some difficulty obtained the military's approval for the new policy.

* Fall, *op. cit.*

Although the plan won the enthusiastic support of the administration in Washington, which accorded it the highest priorities, preparations for its full implementation dragged on for almost a year. By December 1961, when the plan finally went into effect, morale throughout Vietnam had fallen to a critical level.

One is tempted at this point to answer the question: how effective has the plan proved in practice? But to do so now, it seems to me, would be to condone the superficiality that has consistently characterized our approach to the entire problem of unconventional war. First it is essential to examine the basic characteristics and fundamental principles of guerrilla operations and only then to apply them to the current war in Vietnam, as I shall attempt to do in the final chapter. At this stage, the important fact to be underscored is the inability of otherwise competent officials to recognize and react appropriately to the storm signals so conspicuously flaunted by the Vietcong ever since the American advisers had replaced their French predecessors.

Long before the Americans went into Vietnam, the French had discovered to their dismay that Ho Chi Minh's forces invariably refused to fight conventional war and engage in set-piece battles with the professional French battalions until their forces had achieved at least local superiority. It should therefore have been apparent that the Vietcong would not oblige the Americans any more than they had the French.

Indeed, had the American military advisers put themselves for a moment in Ho Chi Minh's shoes, it would have been obvious to them that he had no choice but to resort to unconventional warfare. The French campaign had demonstrated time and again that for the Vietminh to field even a small division in the rugged terrain across the Seventeenth Parallel would have required at least 40,000 porters. Such a supply column would have been at the mercy of the Americans, who had virtual monopoly of the air. In contrast, the infiltration of a few thousand irregulars who could live off the country was the cheapest kind of operation he could undertake. It had proved eminently successful in wearing down the French will to hang on to their possessions and there seemed little reason for the Vietminh to suppose that it would prove less successful in wearing down the Americans. And even if it failed, Ho Chi Minh could disavow the entire operation with a minimum loss of face.

Since the real threat, therefore, was not a frontal attack by divisions across the Seventeenth Parallel but a guerrilla operation, the force to meet it was not army corps but small counterinsurgent units. In the last years of their struggle the French had learned to fight the guerrillas with small commando groups on land and small flotillas of gunboats on the rivers and canals. But perhaps because the French had developed such tactics, the Americans rejected them. Only a handful of "Special Forces" were organized before 1961 and the French flotillas were completely abandoned. In battle after battle Vietnamese regulars were committed in battalion strength in the unequal fight until a crack anti-Communist paratroop outfit revolted at the stupidity of these tactics and laid siege to the Presidential palace in protest.

Mao Tse-tung in China, the Communists in Malaya and again in Greece and the Huks in the Philippines had repeatedly demonstrated that guerrillas in such areas are largely dependent on the villages for their food, recruits and intelligence. It should therefore have been apparent that the first line of defense was not on the frontier but in every little hamlet scattered throughout the countryside. These defenses had to be manned not by heavy artillery or tanks but by far more sophisticated weapons designed to deprive the guerrillas of village support and sympathy, in the first instances by winning the villagers' loyalty with economic and social assistance and then by protecting the loyal villagers from Vietcong reprisals.

But here too, as we have seen, quite the contrary steps were taken. Economic aid was directed at basic development projects centered in the urban areas. Propaganda was aimed at the urban intellectuals. The village rice farmer was ignored. It is small wonder that the Vietcong in the initial phases of the war found so little resistance when they called upon the villagers for food, medicines and even recruits.

Had the appropriate steps been taken from the beginning both in the military and economic fields, while the Vietcong guerrillas numbered only a few thousand, it is possible, indeed probable, that as the United States military adviser so fatuously reported, the Vietcong would soon have "ceased to be a major menace." As it turned out, having refused to learn through the experience of others the well-established fundamentals of this type of warfare, as outlined in the chapters to follow, we were forced to learn the hard way by our own bitter and costly experience. By then it was almost too late.

11 The Wrong Way

As one would expect at a Philadelphia cocktail party, the conversation was loud, fragmentary and dull. Among the guests a local newspaperman wandered from group to group listening with half an ear and replying to stereotyped remarks with equally meaningless answers. By chance he found himself in a group surrounding a small, swarthy, neatly dressed man who was talking volubly in heavily accented English.

After listening to him for some minutes, the newsman asked an acquaintance who the little man was. His acquaintance said he was a consul from some South American country, he had forgotten just which.

Later when he returned home, the newspaperman could scarcely remember a single remark made during the whole hour he had spent at the cocktail party—except what the swarthy little South American had said. But that sounded so weird, almost sinister, that he could not get it out of his head. Was it sensational gossip or was it true?

He and millions of other Americans had the answer on Monday morning, April 17, 1961, when their radios blared out the news of the Cuban invasion.* A few hours before, at one A.M. to be exact, a fleet of old vessels, including four cargo ships, two tank landing craft and a number of small auxiliary vessels, were standing off the southern coast of Cuba. Then a group of frogmen slipped silently over the sides and swam ashore where they set up lighted beacons and markers. Two hours later the first two battalions of the miniature army hit the beach. Simultaneously 175 paratroopers were dropped several miles inland with equipment to blow up the access routes along which Castro could be expected to bring up the defending forces.

The invaders met little resistance in the first hours, for by good luck the time and place of the landing had been kept secret from Castro.

Having landed at two points on the Bay of Pigs, the landing parties quickly linked up. With five tanks they soon overcame several local outposts and moved inland. By the end of the day they had driven nearly twenty miles into the island.

When news of the invasion reached him that morning, Castro was in Havana. He was hardly surprised. For months dozens of his secret agents in Miami had been reporting to him that an expeditionary force was being readied and equipped. Two days before, several old bombers bearing the forged markings of his own air force had bombed and strafed his airfields, but failed to knock out a single one of Castro's operative aircraft, which included two jet training planes, two Sea Furies and a couple of obsolescent B-26's.

* In examining the operation at the Bay of Pigs, it is not my intention to retell in detail the whole sad tale nor to point the finger of blame at any individual or group responsible for it. The first task has been admirably accomplished by Messrs. Tad Szulc and Karl E. Meyer in their detailed account, *The Cuban Invasion*. The second task has been undertaken in innumerable newspaper and magazine articles published after the failure of the invasion. My sole purpose is to illustrate the key problems and decisions that face those who in future may have to undertake a similar operation or to oppose one.

It was obvious to him that the air attack was the preliminary to a landing. He promptly alerted his 30,000-man army and his militia—a force totaling a quarter of a million men equipped with tanks, several batteries of 37 mm. cannon and 120 mm. howitzers.

When the local commander near the Bay of Pigs radioed news of the landing Castro moved his troops by road and rail to the invasion area. He ordered his half dozen planes to ignore the landing forces and concentrate on the invasion fleet.

The invaders had planned a second strike against the Cuban airfields, but the first abortive air assault had raised such a storm in the United Nations and elsewhere that the second strike was canceled. Castro's six remaining planes, concentrating on the ships off the Bay of Pigs, soon had inflicted serious, indeed fatal, damage. A Sea Fury had struck the key vessel, the *Houston,* a 3,000-ton cargo ship which carried much of the reserve ammunition, the reserve battalion of invaders, the key signal equipment and Captain Manuel Artime, the military commander of the expedition. After being hit in the bow, the *Houston* ran aground on a sandspit two miles from the beach and was for all practical purposes eliminated from the action. Meanwhile other airplanes had accounted for one of the landing craft and a number of smaller ships. Soon the men on shore were on their own with no means of resupply, no hope of re-enforcements and no way of retreat.

For some unexplained reason the paratroopers sent to blow up the causeways leading to the beachhead had failed in their mission and within twenty-four hours of the first landing, Castro had brought up his troops and heavy equipment and began to deploy them around the perimeter of the little force. All next day, Tuesday, the howitzers and cannon pounded the invaders, slowly forcing them to retire.

Then the invaders' ammunition began to run short, but with their only reserves stuck on a sandspit two miles from shore, there was nothing to be done. "If only we had more ammunition," one of the fighters later complained, "we might have held out—maybe even won."

By early on Wednesday, the third day of the invasion, Castro moved in for the kill, and by mid-afternoon the invasion force was a scattered band of fugitives. Some had surrendered. A few had escaped in small boats to be picked up by the remnants of the invasion fleet fearfully hovering far off shore, out of reach of Castro's handful of planes. Still fewer had managed to slip through Castro's encircling forces and make their way to the hills in the interior. There one of them set up a small radio transmitter and as the invasion came to its tragic end, a pathetic message was picked up in America: "This is Cuba calling. . . . We need help in Cuba." But the help never came.

Why had the invasion failed? Let us begin with the purely military reasons put forward by dozens of critics and analysts in the public post-mortem that quickly followed in the press. Perhaps the most widely publicized criticism of the Cuban operation was that the White House had ordered the cancellation of the second air strike. Had it destroyed Castro's tiny air force, the invasion forces would have had command of the air and thus been spared destruction. The argument is not convincing. Since the first air strike had been a total failure it is unreasonable to assume that the second would have been a total success. Furthermore, even with air superiority, it is a question whether the 1200 men landed at the Bay of Pigs with five tanks could have withstood the assault of Castro's army of 30,000 plus his militia equipped with 120 mm. howitzers.

It has been argued, too, that to have loaded all the signal equipment, the greater part of the ammunition and the high command on a single vessel was a military error. But even had the *Houston* gotten ashore, it is again a question whether it would have made the crucial difference in the one-sided struggle at the beachhead.

The failure of the paratroopers to blow up the causeways has also been cited as a military mistake. Had they succeeded, they might have delayed Castro's forces from attacking for a few hours. But would this have been long enough for the invasion force to establish itself and recruit re-enforcements among the local population they had expected would flock to them and reverse the balance of forces on the beachhead?

Here we are entering upon the political aspects of the plan. But before doing so we should perhaps return to that cocktail party in Philadelphia. Castro himself has admitted that the invasion achieved tactical surprise both as to location and to timing. But no one has claimed that he did not know of the impending attack. Not only his agents but most wide-awake Americans around Miami had been well aware for months that an invasion of Cuba was being prepared. The consul at the Philadelphia gathering was only repeating what was common knowledge among the thousands of Cuban refugees who had fled Castro's dictatorship. It is an open question whether an operation of this size could have been organized secretly in a society as free as our own. But it is hardly debatable that without strategic surprise an invasion force so heavily outnumbered could never have established a secure enough base to hold out for any long period of time.

There have been other criticisms of the military planning. The type of training, the rate of training—whether it would have been better to have given the invading troops shorter courses and thus trained more of them—the type and quality of the equipment and other military factors have been cited as causes of failure. But all these arguments have the familiar ring of the ancient jingle:

> For want of a nail the shoe is lost,
> For want of a shoe the horse is lost,
> For want of a horse the rider is lost.

Had none of the military nails been lost, it would still have required a bagful of horseshoes loaded with good luck to bring success to a venture so burdened with other, nonmilitary handicaps. The Cuban invasion was not without successful precedents. Nearly a hundred and fifty years ago Napoleon Bonaparte landed from Elba at Cannes with less than a thousand troops and a few guns. Within twenty days without shedding a drop of blood he had overthrown the newly restored French monarchy. To compare Napoleon's landing with the Cuban invasion may appear ludicrous but it is not without value. Napoleon was the once-beloved exiled emperor who had led France to glory. It is significant that the route he deliberately chose from Cannes to Paris lay through the Dauphiné where the restored nobles were disputing the peasants' titles to lands Napoleon himself had given them. Captain Manuel Artime, the military head of the Cuban venture, was, on the other hand, a young exile who was practically unknown. The political leadership included several who opposed the distribution of land by Castro to Cuba's peasants.

Probably the greatest single handicap in any effort to oust Castro was the fact that he had carried out a successful, popular and in many respects necessary revolution. Any attempt to overthrow him must by definition have been counterrevolutionary and would at least bring into question many of the popular reforms, including distribution of the land, which he had carried out.

But it was also true that his justice was abominable, his affiliation with the Communist world threatening to hemispheric security and his blatant anti-Americanism infuriating. American public opinion was righteously indignant that he should continue to flourish less than a hundred miles off our shores. Both major political parties in the United States were pledged to his elimination.

Furthermore, he had alienated many of his fellow Cubans. The most respected of his own revolutionary colleagues who had fought with him in the hills had repudiated him and fled to America. Diplomats, newsmen, longtime American residents in Cuba reported that a significant proportion of the population remaining on the island was ready to rise against him. They comprised elements from almost every political faction and shade of opinion. But whether the planners of the operation recognized it or not, this very fact posed the first key question about the feasibility of the entire enterprise: did Castro's opposition have enough common purpose to forge the unity of effort any such undertaking would require?

Anyone who has had to cope with exiled groups, whether from Poland or Hungary or Korea, knows the difficulty of bringing them together under strong, effective leadership. Old and respected politicians, once in exile, lose their party organizations, their press and patronage and all the other accouterments of political life that had held their followers together at home. And freed from the restrictions of public opinion, every other exile has an equal opportunity to found a political movement or group —and usually does. Before the Russian Revolution even the Communists in exile bound together by the Marxian doctrine were constantly torn by schisms.

The Cuban exiles were no exception. They included Right-wing adherents of the ousted dictator Batista, dedicated to restoring the order that had existed under him with all its inequities of absentee landlords and an impoverished peasantry. They included moderate politicians who deplored equally the antidemocratic methods of Batista and Castro. Among them were former adherents of Castro himself who advocated the continuation of the reforms he had instituted without the political, judicial and social excesses he had resorted to when he came to power.

But not one of them had the prestige or ability to bring all the exiles together. If they were to be united in an effective political movement, it was obvious that their American sponsors would have to play the role of matchmaker. How to accomplish this was the problem. One alternative would have been to select the individual who in American opinion seemed best qualified and let it be known that those who wished to share in the substantial assistance, financial and otherwise, that the Americans were prepared to furnish would have to subordinate themselves to the selectee's command. This method was rejected on the ground that is smacked too much of American interference and dictation. Furthermore, it was recognized that the person who in American opinion might seem best qualified might well not qualify from the Cuban viewpoint.

Furthermore, some of the shrewdest exiled politicians foresaw that if the venture were a success, the government thus brought to power would be heavily tainted with the stigma of being agents of Yankee imperialism. Looking to the second round when a government would be selected by popular vote, they preferred to stand aside and wait.

In the end only by applying considerable pressure did the American sponsors manage to bring together in a single movement most of the leaders, wisely excluding only the extreme Right-wing adherents of the ex-dictator Batista. Only some thirty-five ex-Batista soldiers with questionable records succeeded in getting into the invasion army.

But the amalgamation known as the Democratic Revolutionary Front was a highly artificial organization without any genuine political solidarity and with a tendency to fall apart at the slightest provocation. When some Cuban dissidents in Havana founded their own underground Movement of Revolutionary Recovery, composed largely of former Castro adherents who were bent on continuing his original reforms without his drastic methods, the unity of the Front was severely shaken. (The first crack appeared oddly enough within the M.R.R. and culminated in a fracas in Miami before the invasion in which Captain Artime, the chosen military leader, was soundly thrashed.)

Because of the widely divergent programs of the members of this artificially unified Front, it was quite impossible to put forward a program with any specific, positive national aim. The only goal they shared was the wholly negative one of eliminating Castro personally. They were not even agreed among themselves as to how to dispose of him.

The American sponsors of the operation were fully aware of the tenuous bonds that held the movement together. They even foresaw that once Castro was removed political chaos would probably ensue. But this they felt was preferable to the evils of Castro's order. What they failed to evaluate was the fatal effect of this lack of unified purpose on the actual operation itself. Thus the Cuban venture was launched without the essential prerequisites of a popular insurrection: a positive goal and an effective leadership.

The second problem facing the American sponsors stemmed largely from the first. How could the relatively small force to be landed in Cuba spark a successful mass movement against the thirty-to-one odds posed by Castro's army, to say nothing of his militia? The classic solution Castro himself had found was, of course, a guerrilla operation. In the initial planning phases this was seriously considered.

Castro's opponents, many of them ex-comrades from his guerrilla days, had urgently advised that only by such methods could the operation succeed. Their American colleagues appeared to have accepted their advice at first and up to the moment of the landing many of the underground in Cuba still assumed that the counterrevolution would be by multiple landings of guerrillas. They themselves were preparing a wave of sabotage actions to precede the final combat phase. Some anti-Castro elements had actually established themselves in the Escambray mountains and numerous efforts had been made to parachute to them trained radio operators and supplies which they desperately needed.

But these efforts to help the anti-Castro guerrillas and assist them to establish firm bases failed for a variety of reasons largely stemming from the political rivalries within the opposition. Intensely suspicious of the ultimate aims of the exiled groups, the guerrillas on the island were reluctant to subordinate themselves to them by accepting their aid or their agents. Since they were thus deprived of the supplies they needed from abroad, it was relatively easy for Castro to seal them off in the mountain area where they had sought refuge and to starve them out.

Thereafter, the American sponsors had to form another nucleus of guerrillas, establish another base and gradually build up a network of guerrilla bands which could, by establishing contact with the underground in Havana, build up a force that could then be supplied by air.

But the island underground was itself so split into factions, so untrained in clandestine operations and so undisciplined in security procedures that every effort to send in teams to furnish communications and to train it was frustrated and team after team fell into the hands of Castro's counterintelligence forces whose competence and efficiency were growing with alarming speed.

Every guerrilla leader in history has stressed the need for a highly organized, thoroughly disciplined core of dedicated fighters as a prerequisite for a successful guerrilla operation. Romantic idealists who take to the jungle in order to fight despotism and to establish a liberal system of justice and human rights are hardly inclined to administer the kind of harsh justice required to deter the careless from inadvertent lapses of security or to steel the fainthearted from revealing vital secrets under torture. Only after they have suffered costly casualties through the slips or weakness of their own colleagues do they learn the necessity for extralegal methods to enforce discipline among themselves and their supporters among the civil population. In fact it is a question whether a movement based on democratic organization and dedicated to legality can ever be ruthless and cruel enough to impose the brutal discipline a modern guerrilla force demands. The planners in Washington correctly concluded that it would take much time and many sacrifices of men before the island underground could discipline and organize itself to this degree.

In this respect, totalitarian movements have a great advantage. Communism itself furnishes a ready-made program and an almost fanatical religion which condones not only drum-head discipline but cold-blooded terror with which to cope with the careless and to dispose of the traitor. These tools were at the disposal of Castro's counterintelligence but they did not seem to exist in the arsenal of his opponents.

Nevertheless, the sponsors in Washington were deeply committed to some sort of intervention in Cuba. The customary impatience of the American public, daily more exasperated by the failure of Washington to get rid of Castro, must have put heavy pressure on the Americans who were dealing with the situation. The growing efficiency of Castro's police was a major factor urging them to hurry. A third factor was the knowledge that within a few months Communist-trained pilots equipped with Czech-made jet fighters would be in the air. But this could not have brought about the fatal decision on how to effect the intervention. Jet fighters are notoriously ineffective against guerrilla bands and, had the original plan of mounting a guerrilla operation in classical form been adhered to with greater patience and persistence, the Czech fighters would have played a minor role.

There is cause to believe there was still another reason why the classic guerrilla strategy was abandoned. The military advisers of the sponsors doubtless shared the aversion to "irregular" operations which existed—and still exists—among the regulars in the Pentagon.

Though the Revolutionary War and the Indian wars had left a tradition of scouting and individual fighting in the American army, the less glamorous aspects of guerrilla warfare, as I have already suggested, appealed little to the professional soldiers. The guerrilla's foraging and grubbing for food seemed primitive compared to the intricate systems of logistics they had learned. The improvised tactics of small bands contained none of the charm of the set-piece tactical games they had learned at the sand tables of Fort Leavenworth. The unavoidable terrorist methods of guerrillas were in direct conflict with the concept of military chivalry ingrained at the Military Academy and hallowed in its very motto: "Duty, Honor, Country."

The radar and tank, the heavy gun and rocket, the jet plane and even the humble jeep are relatively useless in the jungle fighting of the irregular—the primitive weapons of guerrilla fighting, including knives, spears, shotguns and hand-made bombs, have none of the allure of the expensive hardware of the modern arsenal.

Above all, the sophisticated "politics" of such popular movements were anathema to soldiers brought up to believe that when fighting began politics ended.

For these reasons guerrilla warfare was regarded as something second-rate and degrading for professional officers, a point of view that must have been reflected in the advice they gave the sponsors of the Cuban operation.

At all events, the decision was made to drop the guerrilla operation and substitute a miniature invasion along conventional lines. Somehow it was hoped a spectacular landing of liberating troops would be sufficient to ignite the flame of revolt and rally the population against Castro. In fact, so great was this expectation that along with the first wave of invaders, 4000 extra rifles were sent ashore to arm the newcomers.

In an oft-quoted passage Mao Tse-tung has drawn the analogy of the guerrilla to fish and the civil population among which he lives to the water. Only if the temperature of the water or the state of mind of the "masses" is right can the fish or the guerrilla hope to survive. Here again the sponsors of the Cuban invasion faced a basic decision: was the temperature of the water right to attract the recruits and saboteurs promptly enough to come to the aid of the invaders?

Washington was fortunate in having no difficulty measuring the political temperature in the island. Daily not only refugees but hardheaded newsmen, experienced diplomats and other Americans with long-established contacts and deep knowledge of the island reported to Washington about the state of the opposition to Castro.

This information indicated that among the upper classes and the better educated urban communities the opposition was bitter and increasing. The shortage of imports and the growing economic poverty of the regime had also alienated large sections of the working class.

On the other hand some elements of the population had materially profited from the Castro reforms—principally the peasant class which for decades had lived a sharecropper's poverty-stricken existence. Though their enthusiasm for Castro had fallen from the hysterical height it reached shortly after he overthrew Batista, it was at least questionable whether these elements were ready to take up arms to throw him out.

Furthermore, anti-American feeling, fanned by Castro's propaganda, was strong among many liberal and propertyless Cubans. The slogan "Yankee Imperialism" was not, as many Americans supposed, a baseless calumny; for as Szulc and Meyer brought out in *The Cuban Invasion* animosity toward Americans had deep historical roots on the island. Though Washington had often come to Cuba's aid in hard times with almost prodigal generosity, American business, especially the sugar companies, was closely identified with the landlordism that was the basic complaint of the landless peasantry. Nor had repeated United States intervention in Cuban affairs in the first quarter of the century been obliterated from Cuban memories. An invasion mounted from American bases, no matter how presented, looked to many in Cuba—as in the rest of the world—like a crudely disguised revival of past landings and the Cuban exiles who manned it like buccaneering stand-ins for the United States Marines.

Did all this add up to a reasonable certainty that the political temperature was ripe for a popular uprising essential to the venture's success? Thanks to hindsight, we know the answer now. What, then, was left out of the calculation? Perhaps the enthusiasm of the exiles exaggerated the strength of the local opposition. Perhaps Washington's informants overweighed the importance of the business and propertied elements, with whom they had more contact, as against that of the peasantry, which in the final analysis would have to do the fighting.

Possibly the inherent difficulty of stimulating counterrevolutions was underestimated. The bitterness of the newly dispossessed is invariably louder than the satisfaction of those who have profited. Perhaps the intensity of the political invective of Latin peoples was mistaken for bellicose militancy.

The readiness of an individual to risk all in open revolt is largely determined both by his political simplicity or sophistication and by his personal stakes. The middle-class Cuban was no simpleton politically. Though he had lost property to Castro, he was still far from having nothing to lose, like the Chinese or Malayan peasant.

A decisive factor in anyone's decision to risk his life for a cause must be his chances of success and survival. In fact, a guerrilla recruiting officer's best weapon to persuade a waverer to join the camp is the threat to assassinate him if he doesn't. Had the dissident groups in Havana been summoned to a guerrilla base or hideout in the Cuban mountains, the example of Castro himself might have convinced them that their chance of survival was not unreasonable. But to join the forces on the beachhead at the Bay of Pigs that April morning must have seemed almost suicidal.

The extent to which these factors were ignored in making the final decision to use conventional methods in an unconventional situation may be indicated by the attitude of the sponsors of the Cuban underground. If suspicions about the coolness of the population to the invaders existed, elementary prudence would have called for every effort to raise its temperature. For this purpose the underground movement in Havana would have seemed made to order. Not only could it supply information and sabotage Castro's mobilization but it could disseminate the propaganda and information to arouse the populace.

The sponsors in Washington, however, had concluded that the Havana underground's security was so riddled that they dared not inform it of their plans lest they be leaked out and the operation lose its essential tactical surprise. The underground was therefore kept in complete ignorance.

When news of the landing reached Castro, however, he ordered his army to the beaches and his secret police to round up every potential dissident in Havana. Within a few hours thousands of innocent bystanders were arrested and crowded together in jails, sports stadiums and even theaters. With them were the leaders of the underground, helpless to render any assistance to their colleagues on the beach.

The American officials who planned and executed the operation at the Bay of Pigs were on the whole highly intelligent men whose judgment in other fields had proved superior. Why then had their plan failed so completely?

It would appear that the answer is twofold. Their own experience provided few precedents for solving the highly unconventional problems with which they were faced. Secondly, those to whom they turned for advice, the military, were just as ill-equipped as they to appraise the situation accurately.

It has been suggested that the Guatemalan revolution engineered by Washington provided a precedent. But as Castro had repeatedly warned, and with good reason, Cuba was no Guatemala. Aside from the obvious geographic differences, the Arbenz regime in Guatemala bore little resemblance to the Cuban revolutionary forces and their leaders. Politically it had neither the depth nor the sophistication of Castro's government and hence inspired few of the loyalties—or indeed passions—that pervaded Cuba. With no real political roots, its overthrow differed little from traditional Latin American *coups d'état.* Indeed the failure of the American planners of the Cuban invasion to see the essential difference is itself an indication that they were throughout applying false criteria.

But just what were the proper criteria which applied to the Cuban situation and which should have controlled the decisions of the planners at every stage, from the initial scheme to use exiles to overthrow Castro to the final military blunder of attempting a one-strike conventional landing? We have already indicated some of them in the course of this chapter. Let us now take a closer look at the more crucial characteristics of unconventional warfare as demonstrated in specific cases.

iii The Cause

WHEN THE JAPANESE drove General MacArthur and his troops from the Philippine Islands, the local Communist party in Manila took to the hills and formed guerrilla bands, called Huks, to harass the invaders. Later, when MacArthur returned, they came back out of the jungle for a brief period in an attempt to gain control of the Philippine government formed when the islands were given their independence in 1946. But failing in their effort they went back to the jungle and resumed their marauding tactics.

The Huks' appeal to the poverty-stricken landless peasants was considerable and they soon acquired a sort of Robin Hood reputation. Particularly strong in Central Luzon, they often dominated large areas of the countryside. Their main base was the inaccessible jungle and swampland around Mount Arayat not far from Manila. In 1950 they were so strong that they even threatened to attack Manila itself.

At that critical moment, President Quirino named Ramon Magsaysay, a young, vigorous ex-guerrilla, as Secretary of National Defense and charged him with putting down the Huk rebellion.

Under the new Secretary the tide began to turn slowly against the Huks. But in 1951 large areas, particularly around the provincial town of San Fernando, were still dominated by the Huks based on the slopes of Mount Arayat.

An old peasant who can be called José Balayub had his hut on the outskirts of a peasant village not far from San Fernando. He was a rice farmer, poor, practically landless and obsessed, as most Philippine peasants were, with a bitter hatred of the central regime in Manila. Three times in his life, the Filipinos had been promised their own government. As a boy, José's hero had been Aguinaldo, the revolutionary who tried to wrest independence first from the Spanish and then from the Americans. Though the Americans had promised them a government of their own when they took the islands from the Spaniards they had held on for fifty years despite these pious assurances. When at last in 1946 they made good their pledge and granted independence, José and his compatriots had their third and bitterest disappointment. For the newly independent Philippine regime turned out to be the least satisfactory of all. Far from representing the majority of landless peasants, the politicians in Manila seemed to represent only a handful of hated landlords and unscrupulous businessmen in Manila.

At least that was what the Huks said and José and his fellow peasants saw no reason to disagree. In election after election they had voted for candidates who they hoped might help them. But each time, by resorting to the most corrupt election tactics including flagrant stuffing of ballot boxes, the landlords' friends had held their posts.

But in 1951, a year after Magsaysay had taken over the Defense Department, an election for senators, congressmen and local officials was held which was different. At the request of the

Commission on Elections, the army had supervised the polling and later the counting of the ballots. The results caused consternation among the politicians and surprised even José Balayub and his friends.

A few nights after the election José, having finished his work in the rice paddies, carefully barred the flimsy door of his hut and went to bed. But he could not sleep. It was time, he knew, for the periodic visit of a Huk foraging squad. For years he had been collecting food, medicine and information for the Huks which he had passed on in these nocturnal visits. His own son had joined the guerrillas with his blessing. After all the Huks, like Aguinaldo fifty years before, were the only ones, he had reasoned, who stood up for the peasantry and spoke out against the corruption of Manila and the subservience of the government to the "colonialists" from America.

Toward midnight José heard familiar footsteps outside and his gaunt, old body stiffened. There was a knock on the door but José lay motionless on his rope cot. A voice outside called out his name in a hoarse whisper. But José did not reply.

Impatiently the visitors raised their voices and began pounding on the door. José knew it was no use pretending he was not there so at last he called back and told them to go away. The visitors seemed surprised and in friendly but hurt tones asked what was wrong. Had not José always welcomed them before? Was he now suddenly going to refuse to give them food and let them starve in their camps on the mountain? What would happen to his son? José knew he could never explain but stubbornly he refused to open up. He called to them to tell his son to come home and go back to work in the rice paddies.

The cajoling tones of the visitors turned to anger. They began to hammer on the door with their rifle butts and José knew it was only a question of time before it gave away. He rose from his cot and stood shaking in the middle of the room. Then the door fell in and on the threshold stood the guerrillas. There were three of them, all armed with rifles with bayonets fixed. One of them started forward and raised the butt of his rifle. That was all José remembered until he woke up in the Army hospital in San Fernando.

Around his bed a half dozen friends and relatives stood moaning and sobbing for they suspected José would never survive the bayonet wounds he had received the night before. Behind their heads José saw an American Air Force officer on an inspection tour of the hospital. Feebly the old man asked a friend to fetch the officer. But the American was reluctant to intrude on the sad family scene for he had been told by the doctors that the old man was dying. José, however, insisted and at last the officer came to the head of the bed.

Gasping painfully, José told him what had happened the night before. He also told him why he had refused to help the Huks. In the elections on the previous Tuesday, he said, the candidates he had voted for had actually been elected. At last, he said, he was going to have a government that was for him. The marauding, pillaging Huks were no longer his champions.

The officer, Colonel (now General) Edward Lansdale, is at present in the Pentagon and loses no opportunity to tell this story of how Magsaysay beat the Huks with ballots.

It is high time. For in American military circles the view is still widely held that guerrillas are just bandits who can be handled only with bullets. This tradition goes back half a century to the Aguinaldo guerrillas, whose insurrection after the Spanish-American War gave the United States Army its first experience with guerrillas since the American Indians were rounded up on their reservations.

How the Army reacted to the job then can be illustrated by the fate of Company "C" of the Ninth United States Infantry. On September 28, 1901, the Company was stationed at Balanga on the Island of Samar where it had recently been sent to clean up the guerrillas. The sixty-nine officers and men of the company were enjoying breakfast that morning at their camp in the jungle. They had had no previous experience with irregulars, knew little about their tactics and after a long period of garrison duty in China were naïvely unaware of the dangers the "bandits" could inflict on regular soldiers.

The night sentries had been withdrawn and the company commander apparently saw no need to replace them during daylight hours. The men had stacked their weapons on one side of the camp and were crowded around the field kitchen when the guerrillas struck from the jungle. Of the sixty-nine officers and men, twenty-four managed to escape and make their way back to base. Forty-five were massacred.

The consternation which news of the massacre on Samar caused at United States Army headquarters in the Philippines quickly turned to indignation and rage. General "Jake" Smith was ordered to proceed to the Island of Samar and "kill everything over ten years old." Apparently General Smith did his best to carry out his mission for when news of his activity reached Congress he was promptly recalled and court-martialed for his brutality. Not until more sober and humanitarian methods were adopted was the Philippine insurrection finally put down.

Magsaysay himself did not rely exclusively on ballots. When he took charge of the anti-Huk operations he described his strategy toward the Huks as offering the fist of all-out force or the hand of all-out friendship.

Up until then, counterinsurgent operations had been directed by a lethargic high command and a halfhearted constabulary using traditional, conventional tactics. Troops and police were concentrated in static positions defending towns and important villages, and only when a particularly outrageous Huk attack compelled them to take action would they "organize" a conventional sweep of the area in which they supposed the Huks were hiding. These sweeps were carried out with all the formality and prior planning of a major operation as taught in the command and staff schools. There were jump-off times, phase lines, zones of action and even priorities of support. Had the Huks behaved like conventional troops they would perhaps have been defeated. But instead they behaved irritatingly like guerrillas. When their supporters like José in the towns and villages saw the preparations for a major operation they sent couriers to warn them. Thereupon the Huks hastily dispersed and faded into the landscape or moved off into another area. The results of these model operations, as one who participated in them puts it, were "no hits, some runs and many errors."

Magsaysay began his strictly military operations first by removing ineffective generals and staff officers, reorganizing the military police and then ordering units to quit their static posts and take to the jungle in small units in active pursuit of the Huks.

Mao Tse-tung said of his guerrilla forces: "We retreat when the enemy advances, harass him when he rests, raid him when he is tired and pursue him when he retreats." Though possibly unpopular among the sedentary generals who had commanded the Philippine troops until Magsaysay removed them, this method like most military strategies was hardly new. Twenty-five hundred years ago Sung Tzu, the first military strategist known to history, wrote: "Keep (the enemy) under a strain and wear him down. . . . When the enemy is at ease, be able to weary him; when well-fed, to starve him; when at rest, to make him move."

In the American Indian campaigns of the nineteenth century, it had been the practice of American generals to organize great sweeps against the Indian tribes during the summer months when the weather was favorable for campaigning and to retire to garrisons during the inclement winters. General Crook, one of the most successful American Indian fighters, was among the first to perceive the futility of such methods. In his campaigns against Geronimo, he trained and toughened his troops so that they could fight in any terrain in any weather. Then he set out in pursuit of the Indians, chasing them from one mountain refuge to another until by this relentless strategy he finally broke their resistance.

Magsaysay now adopted this policy of relentless pursuit against the Huks.

When the widow of President Quezon was ambushed and murdered by Huks, Magsaysay ordered a force of 3000 men into the jungle in pursuit. For seven long months they chased the assassins until they could report that every one of the 250 Huks involved in the assassination had been killed or captured.

At the same time Magsaysay's "fist of force" was not above resorting to the same stealthy, cold-blooded and often brutal stratagems the Huks themselves used. Once he was approached by a fearful peasant who told him that several Huks had sought refuge in his hut and refused to leave. The peasant asked for weapons to capture them. Instead Magsaysay gave him a handful of sleeping pills with instructions to put them in Coca-Cola and offer it to the Huks. Afterward, he explained, the peasant would need only an ax to bash their heads in. Some weeks later, returning to the scene, Magsaysay was presented with five mangled skulls.

Magsaysay likewise encouraged his subordinates to dip into the bag of dirty tricks whenever necessary. One of them commanded a garrison town the mayor of which was strongly suspected of being a Huk agent. The mayor, however, vigorously denied it and, lacking proof, the commander could not legally detain him. But by good fortune, his troops one day picked up a Huk courier near the town carrying important and incriminating documents.

The commander saw his chance and at once called a public

meeting in the town square and before the populace warmly congratulated the mayor for providing the information by which the courier was captured. That same night the mayor and his family carrying their household goods crept into the military headquarters and begged for asylum from the reprisals he knew the Huks would carry out against him for allegedly betraying their messenger.

But Magsaysay's decisive measures were not in the military field. "Political activities are the life of both the guerrilla armies and of revolution," Mao had written, and added one of those obiter dicta so dear to Marxists: "In a war of counterrevolutionary [in Marxist jargon, anti-Communist] nature there is no place for guerrilla activities."

Magsaysay's major achievement was to demonstrate that political activities can just as well be the life of a counterinsurgent movement and of the counterrevolutionary as of the revolutionary or Communist. An ex-guerrilla himself, Magsaysay was a natural politician. Perhaps he had read Mao's book. More likely he followed his own political instincts. But for whatever reason, he followed the Chinese Communist-guerrilla's advice and turned its full force on the Philippine Communists.

When he assumed command, the Huks were estimated to have about 12,000 armed guerrillas. Furthermore, it was estimated that of the 17,000,000 Filipinos, at least 1,000,000 actively supported the Huks by providing food, supplies, information and, when necessary, recruits. On the other hand, the Philippine army had about 30,000 troops. Neutral observers at the time estimated that the government itself could count on hardly more than 1,000,000 active supporters. The great majority of the population stood aloof muttering curses on both houses.

Magsaysay knew by experience the old maxim that "it takes twenty soldiers to catch a guerrilla" and that with a ratio of only five to two, his forces were inadequate to defeat the Huks by military action alone. For this reason political action, he concluded, was not only desirable but essential.

Mao divided political activity into three sectors: as applied to the troops, as applied to the people and as applied to the enemy. He stressed the need for political conviction as a means of maintaining discipline among his troops. "The basis for the guerrilla discipline must be the individual conscience. With guerrillas a discipline of compulsion is ineffective." One reason for this is, of course, that in a guerrilla band the individual soldier cannot be subjected to barrack-yard discipline as in conventionally organized units. Much of the time he is on his own and alone. His combat behavior is seldom under the watchful eye of his commander.

Moreover, while in any army the rigors and risks of campaigning put a strain on the loyalty of the soldier, in guerrilla combat where the rigors are far greater, where food and weapons are scarce and comforts nonexistent, the demands of loyalty are correspondingly higher. Similarly, among outlawed guerrillas the opportunities for banditry, looting, rape and even desertion and betrayal are far higher than among conventionally organized units.

As Mao suggested, Magsaysay began his political action among his own troops.

When he assumed command, their morale and discipline was anything but good. After dismissing the incompetent, corrupt, lax and lazy senior officers he set about restoring morale by handing out rewards and promotions to capable, resourceful officers and soldiers alike. With a phenomenal energy that wore out his aides, he visited his garrisons and camps and participated in actual combat operations. By these frequent unheralded appearances he gradually won the loyalty and restored the self-confidence of his troops.

But when he took over an even more serious handicap than the lack of morale and discipline among his troops was the catastrophic state of relations between them and the civilian population. The regular troops who had been engaged in anti-Huk operations and subjected day and night to ambush, sniping and bombing were understandably suspicious of the population in Huk-infested areas and not unnaturally inclined to consider all of them potential assassins. Consequently they treated the civilian population with ruthless brutality whenever a clash occurred and subjected villagers in disaffected areas to the harshest and most callous treatment when attacked.

The population reciprocated their attitude in full. Considering the troops as hired assassins of the landlords and an oppressive government, they cheerfully protected the Huks and whenever possible harassed the government forces.

An eyewitness of that period has described a truckload of soldiers drawing into a village in broad daylight. The troops stand in the truck, their rifles at the ready, and glare menacingly at the innocent villagers, ready to shoot at the slightest movement that might mean a hand grenade or a pistol shot. The peasants, equally hostile, stare up at the soldiers, taking careful note of their numbers and equipment so as to be able to inform their friends and relatives among the Huks of the new arrivals.

Magsaysay knew that he could make no progress against the guerrillas unless this attitude could be changed. To use Mao's favorite analogy, he had to make the temperature of the water among the populace favorable to his troops and unbearable for the Huks. By every imaginable means he hammered into his soldiers the idea that they must make friends among the local population. He equipped his patrols with medicines and medicos and instructed them to treat any sick peasant they might run across. He also ordered them to help the peasants repair their roads and bridges, to help build schoolhouses and playgrounds for their children and to mingle with them as friends and helpers whenever possible.

Going more deeply into the population's resentments, he pressed President Quirino to dismiss lax officials in Manila and campaigned incessantly in Parliament against the prevalent corruption in and out of government. He ordered the army to provide legal counsel to peasants involved in tenancy cases with landlords and to interfere whenever the course of justice turned against them.

His greatest single action to win over the active support of the population was to guarantee the honesty of national and local elections. The election of 1949 which had installed the Quirino government had been notoriously crooked. Not only had votes been openly bought but election rolls had been padded with names of "dead souls" and children and even with names of flowers and trees. Voters had been openly threatened at polling places and ballot boxes stuffed to such an extent that the number of ballots often far exceeded the voting population.

In 1951, as we have noted, the Philippine electoral commission requested him to assure an honest poll at the bi-annual elections. Thereupon he stationed his own troops at the polling places to maintain a close eye on the ballot boxes and see to it that the ballots were fairly counted. The results of this action, as José Balayub demonstrated, were immediate and marked a decisive turning point in the war against the Huks.

Following Mao's formula, Magsaysay also directed his activities directly to the enemy. He began by offering the Huks and their supporters rewards and outright bribes for information on their activities. One of his very first attempts—ridiculed at the time by his political colleagues—was to persuade a Communist official to betray a meeting of the top Communist officials. As a result he was able to arrest the key underground leaders in Manila and captured invaluable records and rolls. By this one stroke, he deprived the Huk bands of their leadership and vital urban base in the capital. Similarly he offered amnesties to deserters and paid substantial bounties for all weapons turned in—with no questions asked.

Perhaps the most effective of Magsaysay's measures against the Huks themselves was his answer to their persuasive appeal of "Land for the landless." With great effort he managed to persuade the government and the legislature to provide funds and authorization to reclaim fertile areas both in Luzon and on Mindanao, the second largest Philippine island, for a resettlement project to be carried out by an Economic Development Corps which he established within the army.

Army engineers and organizers equipped with tractors, bulldozers and power shovels attacked these jungle areas, cutting roads, driving wells, building community houses and schools and playgrounds and clearing the land for cultivation. Then he offered any Huk who might surrender a plot of land of his own.

The Communist leadership within the Huk ranks realized at once that this offer would undermine their most effective slogan and drain away their adherents. With every means at their disposal they attacked the plan as a trick and fraud. But little by little the Huk rank and file, tired of being hunted like fugitives, began to desert, and after every desertion news trickled back to the jungle hide-outs that E.D.C.O. was no myth but a reality.

In May 1954, four years after Magsaysay had started his campaign against the Huks, their leader, Luis Taruc, finally surrendered. By then the Huks' active combatants had dwindled to a few thousand and their million supporters among the peasantry had locked their doors to the foragers. The Huk rebellion was to all intents and purposes over. The Communist effort was once more driven underground where it still languishes virtually impotent.

Mao Tse-tung has been called the master strategist of Communist guerrilla warfare. Magsaysay might be considered the master strategist of anti-Communist counterinsurgency. His defeat of a Communist liberation movement by eliminating its cause and thus destroying its support demonstrates again the vital importance of the cause or the goal to every insurgent movement. With leadership, it forms what Clausewitz called its "center of gravity."

However, the goals of an insurgent movement are not always identical with those of the Huks. Nor are they often as easily eliminated.

The traditional or historic "cause" of the guerrilla has been to repel or harass an invader. The first guerrillas to use the name were the Spaniards who fought in bands against Napoleon's invading armies. Mao's guerrillas were inspired principally by a determination to rid China of the invading Japanese and only secondarily to establish a Communist regime. The Russian Partisans fought not primarily to defend the Soviet system but to drive the invader from the soil of Mother Russia. The French Maquis, the Polish underground Home Army, the Chetniks and Partisans of Yugoslavia all started as nationalist bands directed against an invader.

However, not all guerrilla movements are of this type. Frequently they rise up against an internal foe—the established regime. For purely political reasons an insurgent movement can spring up to defend or re-establish political rights as the Poles and Hungarians revolted in 1956. On economic grounds a movement for land for the landless frequently develops in predominantly agricultural countries as in the Huk rebellion. In industrialized countries working conditions can drive the populace to rise against the government as the East Berliners rose against the Communists in 1953. The cause may be religious as in the Vendée revolt after the French Revolution or racial like the Jewish uprising in Warsaw or the American Indian guerrilla bands of the last century.

Rationally, whatever the cause, it must be both plausible and compelling. It must invoke a vision of life after the struggle that can sustain the lonely young guerrilla's morale as he lies cold and hungry in a mountain cave. It must overcome his fears when he undertakes a hazardous mission alone and against odds.

It must also possess a high moral appeal that justifies violations of traditional norms of behavior when the young guerrilla is sent out to assassinate in cold blood a rival, an enemy or an innocent bystander. A cause inspired by lust for power, by a clique or simply for loot will enlist only the mercenary, the outlaw and the criminal.

For the less bold noncombatant supporter on whom the fighters rely for food, supplies and vital information it must also justify the risk of enemy reprisal to himself and his family if the adversary discovers his treachery.

The cause must appear to be unachievable by less violent means. For only if the political or legal system seems to deny redress will the risks of violence be acceptable.

Finally, no matter how right the cause may seem, unless it has some hope of fulfillment and unless its champion has some chance of survival, no one but the fool, the suicidal maniac or the fanatic will risk his life for it.

History, however, provides few examples of a cause which has attracted popular support for such purely rational reasons. The fact is that every insurgent movement has a large element of the irrational. Fanatical nationalism, extreme frustration with prolonged social or political injustice and the madness of revenge are among the most frequent emotional motives of guerrilla violence in civilized communities. In more primitive societies, such as the Kikuyu, even less rational motivations provoked by witch doctors and medicine men can start movements like the Mau Mau.

In addition to inciting to violence, a cause must be capable of disrupting traditional or historic loyalties. In civilized countries these loyalties may be to a nation, a system or government or even to a single political party (not necessarily Communist). But in less developed regions loyalties are frequently confined to the family, tribe or community. The villager whose only direct contact with the central regime is the periodic visit of the tax collector in normal times or the relief director in times of famine has only a superficial or at best a traditional veneration for the central authority.

In World War II, for example, the French Maquis often displayed heroic loyalty toward a symbol, hardly more than a philosophic concept of a system which held out the hope of a future life. The villagers of South Vietnam, however, find it difficult to give their loyalty to the central regime in Saigon not necessarily because it displeases them but because they simply cannot identify the interests of their village with that of the remote central government.

In such areas, the attitude of the villagers toward a guerrilla band or a counterinsurgent force will be determined largely by the treatment they receive from it. In his treatise on guerrilla warfare in China. Mao Tse-tung laid down precise rules for his troops' behavior toward the civilian population, including such details as not bathing in front of women and not taking food without compensation.

Magsaysay, as we have noted, realized that his troops could not carry out successful counterinsurgent operations unless their relations with the local population were vastly improved by civil assistance.

"Civic action," as it is called, has a dual purpose. The most immediate is to make its practitioners more popular among the population so that they can operate without fear of betrayal and acquire an invaluable source of information against the enemy. In this sense "civic action" can work for either the guerrilla or the counterinsurgent.

In another, more profound sense, civic action tends to demonstrate the concern of the central regime represented by its troops for the welfare of the masses and thus to strengthen the loyalties of the villagers to the authorities. When performed by outsiders, for example by American liaison officers in Laos or Vietnam, it loses this effect and, while it may make the officers more popular, demonstrates only the bountifulness of the foreigner. Hence even when civic action is undertaken by foreign liaison staffs it must be made to appear the work of the native authority and not of the generous outsider.

As we have seen "civic action" can take many forms. Both Mao and Magsaysay appreciated the particular effectiveness of doctors and medicine among backward villagers. Mao instructed his guerrillas to familiarize themselves with folk medicine in the event Western medicines were unavailable for the treatment of the civilian population. As we have noted, Magsaysay sent army doctors with his counterinsurgent forces with precise instructions to assist the civilian sick.

Whereas the cause of a genuine, indigenous movement and that of a Communist-led "liberation war" have much in common, they also have fundamental differences. For the first the cause is the ultimate aim. For the Communist the cause is a means to an end—the establishment of a Communist regime.

The essential prerequisite of both a genuine movement and the synthetic Communist liberation war is the existence of a grievance which is either real or can be made to appear real to the rank and file. The genuine movement fights for the removal of the grievance. The synthetic movement exploits it to attract support. In a Communist-led movement the professed cause may in reality be utterly unobtainable—such as the get-industrialized-and-rich-quick promises of Communist movements in Southeast Asia. But this is of little concern to the leadership for, long before the promise comes due, it plans to have full control over the population through the coercive powers of a political police force. As we have noted, the Marxist-Leninist doctrine is, of course, ideally suited to arousing the passions of suppressed peoples. From the Manifesto of 1848 to the latest pronouncements of Khrushchev, Communist teaching is deliberately designed to foster militant action against non-Communist regimes.

Furthermore, the secretive conspiratorial nature of the Communist Party both in Moscow and in its agencies throughout the world provides an excellent organizational structure for directing such mass movements, complete with a central headquarters and trained cadres to prepare the groundwork before the combat phase, to control operations during the combat and finally after victory to establish the Communist dictatorship.

Like all Communist operations, "liberation wars" take two basic forms. Some are avowedly Communist and proclaim the dictatorship of the proletariat as their aim. Just as frequently they profess outwardly and toward their rank and file to be non-Communists and operate under such slogans as agrarian reformers. They play down or try to hide completely their Communist sympathies and their connections with the Communist international movement.

Mao, for example, as we have seen, professed that the goal of his movement was "driving out Japanese imperialism and establishing a free and happy China." He even urged his guerrillas to distribute the Kuomintang pamphlet on national organization. His ultimate aim, however, was by no means the re-establishment of the Kuomintang system but the imposition of a Communist dictatorship.

The fundamental appeals of Communism to those who join avowedly Communist movements or to those who are taken into the hard-core center of a cover-organization vary immensely from area to area and class to class. In England and the United States, for example, those who join are apt to be persons unable to adjust to their community life. In Italy and France, many join out of genuine protest against existing political inadequacies—because other parties do not represent their ideas of social or economic progress.

In an excellent study of the appeals of Communism to the people's liberation movements of Southeast Asia, *Guerrilla Communism in Malaya*, Lucian W. Pye has carefully studied the motives which attracted the Malay Chinese to Communism and subsequently made them reject it. He suggests that many Malayans joined the Party just as other people join the government service. Viewing Communism as the system of the future, they sought to enhance their private fortunes and careers by joining it just as a young American might join the Foreign Service.

Whatever its appeals and organizational advantages, the Communist movement also labors under handicaps which make it far from the invincible conspiracy it professes to be and is often considered to be by its enemies. For one thing, the secrecy of its operations and finances and its own inner cynicism make it peculiarly susceptible to infiltration by opportunists and charlatans. Southeast Asian Communist parties have been riddled by swindlers who have walked off with their funds and their secrets.

But more important, since its doctrine is rigid but its policies are based less on principle than on local expedients or on the current requirements of the center in Moscow, it is vulnerable to heresies which divide its leadership and destroy its unity and the discipline essential in guerrilla operations.

Its greatest defect would appear to be the fleeting nature of its charms. Its abrupt reversals of policy to conform to the requirements of the Soviet Union frequently disillusion Western intellectuals. Its failure to provide advancement and better social status for the Malay careerist, Pye discovered, disenchanted many recruits after only a year and a half or two years of service.

Those whom it manages to retain for life are often prevented from deserting only by the intolerance of the non-Communist societies in which they live. They are like the detribalized askaris of Africa who manned the colonial forces of the British and Germans in Africa before World War I. The askaris, by joining the colonial armies, forfeited their rights and position within the tribe. Thus, unable to return home with honor, they spent their lives in military service. Similarly, the drones of the Communist parties in many areas are just as likely to be spiritually homeless waifs as fanatical zealots.

An important weapon for combating these handicaps of the Communist movement is fear. The use of terror as a weapon by the guerrilla or counterinsurgent is the subject of a separate chapter. Here it is only necessary to mention that indoctrination by fear is a standard practice of Communist guerrilla warfare. Implacable foes are assassinated; waverers are kidnaped or killed; deserters are liquidated. Thus encouraged by the fate of its enemies those caught up by the movement find security for themselves and their families a formidable argument to remain loyal to its cause.

How does one go about combating an effective cause, be it a genuine indigenous one or a synthetic Communist liberation war? Some military specialists have suggested that the best way to deal with guerrillas is to prevent the grievances or discontentments which make them take to the woods. This advice, however, reminds one of the doctor's prescription for insomnia: get plenty of sleep.

Discontentment is too often inevitable and unavoidable in the present fast-changing world. Furthermore, as we have indicated, where no real grievances exist, it is sometimes possible to create them. As the Russian proverb says: "When there is no fish, crayfish will do."

Basically there are two ways of handling guerrilla uprisings: wise politics or a strong police. Magsaysay has provided an example of the first type. (In another chapter we shall examine another variant of the Magsaysay approach: where the insurgent cannot be isolated from his support ideologically, physical isolation may be possible, as in the case of the Malayan Communists.) The distinguishing feature of this method is to defeat the insurgent without sacrificing the normal restraints of popular government. Since it was often impossible for Magsaysay's troops to collect adequate legal evidence against suspected insurgents, he was constrained to suspend the right of habeas corpus and hold suspects without permission of the courts. But with this exception which he used sparingly, the Philippine Constitution with all its guarantees of civil liberties remained in force throughout the conflict.

The second method of dealing with guerrillas is through brute force without regard to constitutional or other legal or ethical restraints. Justifying its brutalities under the slogan of fighting fire with fire, it has an especial appeal to those whom Mao calls "simple-minded militarists" as well as to those for whom civil rights have little meaning.

It is the method employed by the Russians in Berlin in 1953 and again in Budapest in 1956. Basically it is the approach Chiang Kai-shek used against the Communists in the 1930's and which the French employed against the Vietminh and again against the Algerian rebels. In the name of stability it is a favorite approach of military dictators in Latin America and elsewhere.

The pattern is familiar. When a popular uprising or guerrilla movement develops to the combat phase, the entire police and military force is directed not only against the guerrilla combatants but against all elements which can be suspected of supporting or even sympathizing with the movement. Using reprisal and terror indiscriminately, without judicial restraints, it can if it strikes early and vigorously enough halt the movement.

The method has two drawbacks. To be in a position to strike a timely blow it must depend on an efficient, powerful political police and intelligence system. Such a system is costly both in manpower and in the limitations it imposes on popular civil liberties. It cannot tolerate any laxness or complacency that might allow a guerrilla conspiracy to organize cadres, caches of arms or hide-outs. Thus far, the Soviet system alone has been able to afford this luxury to the extent that a successful uprising of the discontented satellites is virtually impossible.

The second handicap is its impermanence. Instead of mitigating grievances to the point of toleration, it tends to aggravate them. Those who might have spurned resorting to force, despite their frustrations, tend to become more frustrated so that the potential civilian support for a mass movement and the potential recruits for guerrilla bands grow.

While the advantages of the wise-politics method over the strong-police method are self-evident, it must be borne in mind that a program of modernization and reform is not always a sure preventive against mass movements. Indeed, even a popular government can under some circumstances become the victim of a cleverly controlled minority mass movement. Modernization and industrialization are costly both in an economic and a spiritual sense. In their early stages they call for material sacrifices and difficult psychological adjustments which are easily exploitable by Communists aiming at disrupting the country or by conservatives opposing all change. Occasionally we even find the paradox of extreme conservatives aiding and abetting Communist movements in order to block reform.

The Cuban guerrilla, Che Guevara, argues that land reform is the most common and popular issue of guerrillas in the modern world. But every system of land tenure has its supporters as well as its detractors. The more prosperous peasants and primitive agriculturalists, bound by custom and tradition, are often as opposed to land reform as the large landholders.

The history of land tenure in western Europe has often been compared to an accordion constantly expanding and contracting.

A revolution distributes land to the poor in small, uneconomical, inefficient plots. The more successful or lucky peasants gradually take over the fields of the less successful. Thus the size of the holdings increases and the number decreases. Finally, another reform redistributes the land and the process begins anew.

Critics of Diem's counterguerrilla war in Vietnam suggest that he cannot win until he adopts more thoroughgoing land reforms. His supporters argue that his land reform program is entirely adequate and that the security of the villagers rather than the land tenure system is the critical factor in the struggle against Communist guerrillas.

Since a large proportion of any population is usually politically inert, it will throw its support and favor to that side in a guerrilla war which provides it the greatest personal security and allows it to continue its normal routines with the least interference or interruption. In short, the side which can promise its friends the greatest protection—and its enemies the greatest harassment—will gain the largest share of support from the otherwise neutral mass.

This proposition, however, applies only to those who hold themselves aloof because they consider themselves unaffected by the issues at stake. Thus we come back to our original proposition that the cause which attracts the greatest following is likely to be the winner. But to accomplish this, it must be effectively propagated among the otherwise neutral mass, for a cause, no matter how forceful in other respects, can only attract by becoming known. This is the task of the propagandist.

Prior to World War II propaganda, the business of encouraging friends, persuading neutrals and deceiving enemies was considered by professional soldiers as a deceitful and ignoble operation. However, successful generals throughout history have thought better of it. "All warfare," Sung Tzu wrote twenty-five hundred years ago, "is based on deception."

With the extension of total war to its limits in World War II, propaganda came into its own albeit under the more respectable name of "psychological warfare." General Eisenhower is often quoted as saying that "psywar" was worth six divisions during his European campaign. After the war when the guerrilla units were abolished, psywar was retained in the American forces and subsequently became the nucleus of the new special warfare units.

The French army, smarting under its bitter experiences in the Indochinese war, was the first to make a serious study of modern psychological warfare methods and to elevate it to a science. It divided propaganda into two aspects: psychological war and psychological action. The first comprised propaganda operations directed against the enemy, the second toward friends or neutrals. As practiced by the French in Indochina and Algeria, psychological war used every instrument of persuasion from the truncheon to brainwashing.

American psywar practice more fastidiously confines itself to leaflets, loudspeakers and radios, and the practitioners themselves tend to operate along the lines of advertising specialists and public-relations experts.

There is no doubt that properly evaluated and properly conducted propaganda is an exceedingly useful weapon in all military operations. In irregular warfare, where public opinion is "the center of gravity," it is indispensable.

However, perhaps because it is often associated with advertisers accustomed to selling their products, propaganda has a tendency to be oversold itself. It is often suggested that trained Communist agitators are so skillful at mob psychology that they can cause revolutions by propaganda alone while the Western world, ignorant of this science, stands by helpless. In their zeal to prove the superiority of Communist crowd manipulators some enthusiasts seem to forget the anti-Communist riots in Poznan and Budapest or even the government-sponsored riots against foreign embassies in Moscow which got completely out of hand. One well-known political commentator has proposed the spending of a billion dollars to develop the science of psychological warfare and mob manipulation and to organize skilled cadres to counteract Communist liberation movements.

The fact is that, despite its name, psychological warfare is not a method of war at all but an auxiliary tool. Like an artillery piece it is useless without the proper ammunition. The gadgetry of propaganda—loudspeakers, radios, printing presses—can be operated by any skilled mechanic but their effectiveness is not measured in terms of reams or decibels.

Furthermore, while the creation of a script or leaflet requires considerable skill in the selection of themes and the method of presentation, no script or leaflet, no matter how skillfully composed, can be effective without the proper ingredients. "Public opinion," Clausewitz said, "is ultimately gained by great victories." Without success to propagate, propaganda is a relatively feeble instrument. The resort to the big lie of Goebbels or the demonstrable falsehoods of Communist propagandists is not only incompatible with freer forms of society, but, in the long run, is self-defeating.

Since propaganda must be tailored to the level of the audience, it is rare that pure reasoning or argumentation, no matter how logical, is convincing. In Malaya the British found propaganda useful in their operations against the Communists but only when they had something tangible and convincing to say.

In short, the successful guerrilla or counterinsurgent leader does not overestimate the range of the propaganda weapon. Propaganda without an effective cause behind it cannot of itself ignite a mass movement. The best it can do is help prepare the tinder or fan the flames once ignited. The uprising in Budapest in 1956 was not started by Western broadcasts but by the frustration of the population itself. Thus propaganda is an auxiliary weapon of the irregular or counterinsurgent. It is not a force in itself and is directly dependent on political realities and military events for the ammunition it is designed to deliver.

As the Kremlin itself has occasionally discovered to its embarrassment, effective causes are not often found or easily manufactured. Even when such causes do exist, there remains the problem of overcoming the apathy of the masses, of convincing them that the movement is worth fighting for. Just as difficult, however, is the problem of providing the leadership that can command the loyalty of a following, inspire it to bear the hardships of guerrilla life and preserve the unity without which any mass movement is doomed. Let us therefore take a look at this second center of gravity—leadership.

IV The Leadership

In a spacious peasant house in the village of Brajici on the slopes of Ravna Gora mountain in Serbia, two men were seated facing each other across a large round table. One, the host, sat slightly stooped, his face partly hidden by a gray-brown beard. His eyes behind steel-framed glasses were pale blue and mild. When he spoke his manner was soft and gentle. But behind the soft tones and the mild eyes one could detect the tough, austere bearing of a professional soldier.

His guest was a stocky little man. He was clean shaven and his handsome face also had the cut of a tough, determined individual but it was the toughness not of a soldier but of one who during his forty-odd years had seen the rougher side of life—often in prisons. Though he spoke little, his eyes darted about nervously with a sharp, shrewd look and he listened intently to everything that was said.

Both men evinced an unusual, modest charm and the self-confidence of men who naturally attract a following and as naturally

(51

command respect. Each of them had two aides at his sides and behind them stood their bodyguards, armed with a varied assortment of pistols, knives and rifles, reflecting the distrust each side had for the other. Like their leader the bodyguards on one side wore full, shaggy beards and long hair. The others were clean shaven, younger and less military in appearance. They seemed to take a keen interest in everything that was said and occasionally even butted into the conversation with suggestions of their own which the bearded ones seemed to resent, but which their leader listened to gravely and patiently.

Draja Mikhailovitch, the host with the bushy beard, was a former colonel of the Royal Yugoslav Army and now the commander of the Chetnik guerrillas opposing the German occupation troops. A staunch Royalist, he had been named by the exiled King Peter as Minister of Defense of the Royal Government then in exile in London and was the only representative of the Royal Government left on native soil. His role had been officially recognized by the Western allied governments and on his staff was a young British liaison officer, Captain William Hudson. For some months the BBC had been broadcasting highly romantic stories of his successful exploits and he already enjoyed the reputation of a guerrilla hero throughout the allied world.

His guest, Josip Broz, who called himself Tito, was the head of the Partisan guerrillas and of the Yugoslav Communist party. But he enjoyed no such international reputation or recognition. Even the Kremlin seemed reluctant to recognize its agent. Indeed, few outsiders had ever heard of him and even when he became better known the rumor circulated in allied circles that he was really a woman.

At the time of the meeting there was not much to choose between the strength of their forces. Both were small, ill-supplied and ill-armed. What the Partisans lacked in professional military officers they made up for in youth and enthusiasm. What the

Chetniks lacked in ideological fanaticism they compensated for by their passionate Serb nationalism and devotion to their young King.

Both men were charismatic, natural leaders whose followers were fanatically devoted to them. Among the Chetniks, Draja was almost as much revered as the King himself. Among the Yugoslav Communists, Tito had established a reputation which apparently gave the Father of Communism, Stalin, some qualms.

But with that any similarities between the two ended. Though both were ostensibly equally nationalistic and each professed the aim of liberating Yugoslavia from the Germans, their ultimate goals were totally different. Mikhailovitch's object was to preserve his beloved Serbia and keep together a force that one day could restore the old order of which he was the champion: the Monarchy, the Church and the Serbian way of life.

Ostensibly, Tito professed that the Partisan movement was above political parties. However, he was too ardent a Communist to forget for a moment that his final objective was Socialist revolution, the very opposite of restoration.

The object of the meeting at Brajici which Tito had proposed was to establish some sort of joint command or at least co-operation between the two resistance forces: a joint supply system and joint operations. As he watched the professional soldier opposite him, Tito doubtless felt confident that in the end, in the ultimate political struggle for control of the resistance, Mikhailovitch would fall an easy prey to the sophisticated infiltration tactics of the Communist Party.

Mikhailovitch, on the other hand, saw little advantage in an alliance with Tito's forces. Personally he must have found it distasteful to even have to deal with the former jailbird. Mikhailovitch was a cabinet minister. He had received official promises of aid and arms from the Allies. Tito was the head of an outlawed political party. Besides he seemed to have very grandiose ideas about taking offensive action against the German regulars. As a professional, Mikhailovitch warned Tito that guerrillas could not hope to win against so well-organized a force as the German army.

These negotiations, like those that had preceded them, were fruitless. Tito left disappointed. Doubtless Mikhailovitch was glad to see him go. They never met again.

Five years later, Draja Mikhailovitch, the ex-Minister, crawled from a foxhole near the town of Visegrad on the borders of Serbia where he had been hiding. His last four followers had disappeared. His clothing was tattered and lice infested. His beard, the symbol of his romantic resistance, was matted and filthy. His haggard face and sunken eyes reflected his exhaustion and hunger. It was dark, and slowly and stealthily he made his way to the nearest cottage where he hoped to get some bread. Suddenly he found himself surrounded by a squad of Tito's soldiers and before he could react handcuffs shackled his wrists. Four months later, back at last in Belgrade, he was tried for treason, convicted of war crimes and executed.

How had the legendary Serbian Robin Hood, who had everything in his favor at the time of the Brajici meeting four years before, been so completely defeated by the little blacksmith's son, Tito?

A British liaison officer with Mikhailovitch's forces has pointed out that Mikhailovitch was a professional soldier turned politician whereas Tito was a politician turned soldier. Superficially one might attribute the outcome of their rivalry to this circumstance though the real causes were far deeper.

Ostensibly, as I have pointed out, their aim was the same—to wrest political power from the occupiers and return it to the Yugoslavs. Mikhailovitch made no secret of his ultimate aim of restoring the Yugoslav monarchy. Tito was less specific. When he took to the woods his instructions from Moscow read: "At this stage you are concerned with liberation from Fascist oppression not with Socialist revolution." He therefore welcomed into his movement almost anyone willing to fight the Germans, including even priests, for had he relied on the handful of Yugoslav Communists his movement would have been doomed from the start.

When the meeting took place in Brajici in 1941, the German armies could claim an unbroken record of successes in Europe. Everywhere their troops were advancing. Though Mikhailovitch and Tito both believed that this victorious march would end and that Hitler would ultimately be defeated, 1941 was hardly the time to debate the post-Hitler structure of Yugoslavia. On the contrary, they both preached the necessity for a common effort to stop the German march.

Nevertheless, even at that period neither leader for a moment lost sight of his ultimate goal: the one to restore the monarchy, the other to replace it with a Communist dictatorship. As time went on and the Germans were stopped at Stalingrad and in North Africa and eventually Allied victory became more than a dim hope, their followers too thought more about the postvictory aims and the rivalry between the two camps grew more clear-cut.

Thus from the very beginning each had not only a different aim but a different concept of how best to contend with the Germans. Each, too, had a following which, as the two movements developed, quickly discovered that the way resistance was conducted had a very immediate influence on its own interests.

Initially, as the only known resistance group Mikhailovitch's Chetniks attracted all patriotic Serbs regardless of political views. Their first successful attacks on the Germans so glamorously reported by the BBC and other Allied radios, however, had put their loyalties to an extreme test.

Unreported by the BBC but known to every Serb was the violence of the German reaction—reprisal. For every German soldier and officer killed the occupiers seized scores of men, women and children, usually from among the more prominent townsmen and villagers, and shot them mercilessly. Some reporters stated that a hundred were shot for every German casualty; others put the figure as high as three hundred. Whole villages and towns were razed in districts where the Chetniks had operated. The mildest retributions were collective fines which, naturally, fell most heavily on the well-to-do.

Churchill in hailing the initial Yugoslav revolt had said that the country had "found its soul." But the victims of the Germans' reprisals began to wonder whether souls were much use without homes or even bodies to dwell in. From the outset Mikhailovitch faced the dilemma whether, if he continued to harass the Germans, there would be much left to restore once the occupier was driven out.

As a patriotic Serb he was well read in the heroic exploits of the Serbian guerrillas who had fought the Turks for centuries and he fully appreciated the role the guerrilla could play in a resistance to foreign occupiers. But as a professional soldier, he also knew that no guerrilla band could defeat as well-equipped and organized a force as the German army without the ultimate assistance of outside armies. As a veteran of the Salonika campaign in the First World War, he like most of his officers was obsessed with the strategic advantage if not the necessity of an eventual Allied landing in the Balkans. If he temporarily took the defensive, dispersing his troops to their villages and keeping together only a nucleus staff, he would be ready when the day came to make a valuable contribution to the invading forces by striking in the enemy's rear. But if he continued to harass the Germans, he was reasonably certain that by the time the Allies were prepared to launch a landing there would be no Chetniks left.

These strategic considerations were strongly, probably decisively, supported by his followers in Belgrade and in the provincial towns and villages on whom his Chetnik bands depended for contributions of money and food. The staunchest of his supporters were, naturally, the propertied classes, merchants, established professional lawyers and doctors, rich peasants and leading adherents of the monarchy—in short the "haves."

The Germans were well aware that the Achilles heel of the guerrilla movement is not the elusive guerrilla in the forest but the family and property he leaves at home. They made the most of this circumstance. Thus it was on the propertied classes that their reprisals fell most heavily.

It was effective—against Mikhailovitch. He gave orders that no harassment of the enemy was to take place without his personal consent which he would give only if convinced that its military result was worth the cost of reprisals. Mikhailovitch's perplexed and vulnerable supporters welcomed the decision. Indeed, they probably dictated it by threatening to withhold aid to the Chetniks unless they desisted from reprisal-provoking actions. The government in exile in London likewise supported his decision.

"I call upon you not to start an armed uprising against the enemy occupation forces," its Prime Minister, Slobodan Jovanovic, broadcast to Yugoslavia, "for you would bring upon yourselves severe losses and reprisals and your struggle would not help our Allies. . . . When the right moment comes for an armed fight . . . we shall call on you to rise."

Tito, the politician, decided otherwise. As a revolutionary he had no interest whatever in seeing the old order restored or its adherents preserved. Sir Fitzroy Maclean, who later was head of the British Military Mission to Tito, points out: "He had been fighting the old order all his life and rejoiced at its downfall. He welcomed the opportunity of destroying what remained of it. He was determined to set up a new order in its place, a revolutionary order. That aim bulked at least as large in his aims as the defeat of the enemy."

Hence he refused to be deterred by the German reprisals. His original followers, unlike Mikhailovitch's, were largely from the dispossessed, or the "have-nots," young men without families, the laboring classes, landless farm workers and others who had little to lose from the savagery of the German troops.

To Tito every banker shot in reprisal was one less capitalist to deal with after the Germans were defeated. Every farm burned was one less kulak to liquidate. In fact, the greater the reprisals, the more recruits he could expect from those who were left homeless and without family ties. It has even been suggested that Tito provoked retaliation in order to swell his own ranks.

He was probably as well aware as Mikhailovitch that the damage he caused the enemy was in no way comparable to the destruction they wrought on the innocent civilian population. But this was a total war, a people's war, and everyone, whether he liked it or not, was involved and had to share the risks. Furthermore, with few adherents among the peasantry to feed them voluntarily, Tito's partisans were soon forced to requisition their supplies. In the towns the propertied elements were by nature committed to the Chetniks and not to the Socialists. Hence Tito had few friends to lose by bringing reprisals on the civilian population.

Tito also knew that a static defense such as Mikhailovitch's was fatal to any popular movement. Those who left their homes to fight the Germans did not do so in order to starve in some wretched mountain cave awaiting orders from a foreign invader that the day had come.

British and American liaison officers attached to Mikhailovitch and later to Tito have testified to the bickering and jealousies, the intrigues and quarreling that marked Mikhailovitch's idle command and to the enthusiasm and energy of the Partisans with Tito.

As the war progressed and the tide turned against the Germans, followers of Mikhailovitch and Tito alike began to look into the future to the day when victory would come and began to recognize that the real enemy was not the Germans but the rival guerrilla force. Committed to inaction against the Germans, many Chetniks fell to the temptation of seeking help from the occupiers or their quisling troops in their fight against the Partisans. Though most Chetniks probably spurned all contact with the enemy there is considerable evidence that some actually collaborated with them, thus earning the added hatred of their rivals and the contempt of the civilian population who still regarded the Germans as the chief enemy.

A vital factor in the final outcome was the relative aid in supplies and arms furnished by the Allies to the two sides. In the early days of Mikhailovitch's struggle, the Allies, hard pressed on every front and desperately short of planes, were in no position to fly large amounts of arms to Mikhailovitch's beleaguered guerrillas. Furthermore, British liaison staffs with his forces were reporting continuously that such minor operations as the Allies requested in sabotaging German supply lines were either carried out with the greatest reluctance or vetoed by Mikhailovitch because of the cost in reprisals. In contrast, liaison staffs with the Partisans reported the enthusiasm with which such operations were executed by Tito's forces.

For purely military reasons, the Churchill government finally decided that it would back the force which killed the most Germans. Since the Chetniks were obviously not opposing the occupation and since it was known that the Germans had to keep as many as twelve or thirteen divisions in Yugoslavia, it was obvious who was killing the Germans.

By 1943, the Western Allies, exasperated with Mikhailovitch's policy of no action and impressed by Tito's successes in holding down the many German divisions, withdrew their support of Mikhailovitch and gave their blessing and with it promises of aid to the Partisans. By now they had adequate fleets of long-range planes; their bases in Egypt and later in Italy made supply drops far simpler and their own stores of weapons were far greater than when they had first promised assistance to Mikhailovitch but were in no position to deliver it. Whereas Mikhailovitch had in the course of a year received only a few score drops, now Tito's forces received as many as that in a single night. If any doubt remained as to who was going to rule Yugoslavia cnce the Germans had been driven out, this decision removed it.

It has been argued that the military considerations behind this decision were as shortsighted as Mikhailovitch's and that political considerations—the establishment of a free government in the largest Balkan state after the war—should have dictated withholding aid from the Communist Tito. But were Tito's forces really Communist and dedicated to the overthrow of a free society?

Tito vigorously denied it. Team after team of observers parachuted to him reported that a large proportion of his Partisans were genuine liberals and that at heart Tito was a nationalist reformer whose Communist connections were second to his patriotic loyalties—until the decision had been made.

When finally the Soviet armies entered Yugoslavia, they found a well-armed, well-disciplined Communist Partisan force to greet them—not just scattered guerrilla bands but highly organized units up to division strength. The Chetniks on the other hand were reduced to a handful of desperate outlawed fugitives hiding in the hills.

The Chetnik and Partisan forces have been called the archetypes of guerrillas into which all types of popular rebellions can be divided—the "haves" and the "have-nots," the propertied guerrillas highly vulnerable to reprisal and the dispossessed for whom reprisals have little or no significance. It would be a mistake, however, to assume that either type is invariably Right or Left, conservative or progressive, Communist or anti-Communist.

While the forces of stability and property are in the non-Communist world more often than not conservative, it is quite the other way around in the Communist empire. There the privileged officials, well-paid intellectuals and other propertied elements—in a word those who have something to lose—would be the passive "haves," the Chetniks, so to speak. The "have-nots" would be the laboring class, the collectivized peasants—the dispossessed. Those with least attachment to the Communist Party would be the active Partisans.

In the previous chapter the importance of the cause to every popular movement was discussed. The essential need for a grievance was noted. In the case of Yugoslavia, the cause was nationalism, the grievance foreign occupation both for Tito and Mikhailovitch. The difference was in the ultimate aims of the two leaders.

Generally speaking, it is the leader who determines not only the direction but the method by which the cause is to be achieved, and he interprets the goal according to his own standards and beliefs.

What are the basic characteristics of the successful guerrilla leader? Mikhailovitch was a professional soldier who knew all about the potentialities of guerrilla warfare and how it is conducted. Tito was a professional revolutionary agitator who knew next to nothing about military matters or guerrilla warfare when he took to the hills. Moreover, Mikhailovitch had not only a staff of competent professional officers but most of the weapons of the defeated Yugoslav army which were not captured by the Germans in the initial invasion. To begin with Tito had neither, though subsequently he recruited a number of professional staff officers. Yet the amateur starting with such a handicap against him beat the professional.

The paradox is more apparent than real. Looking over the list of successful modern guerrilla leaders, we find practically none who had previous military experience. Mao Tse-tung was a student and librarian and subsequently a professional trained revolutionary. Ho Chi Minh was a Socialist agitator and his chief lieutenant, Giap, was a French-trained teacher of history. Castro was a lawyer. Ben Bella and Belkacim Krim were noncommissioned officers during the war who turned to politics as soon as they were discharged. The only partially successful guerrilla with professional military training was Georg Grivas of Cyprus, whose movement was devoted practically exclusively to terrorism and was modeled not on what he had learned in military schools but on his study of Communist methods.

In World War I, a German, Lieutenant Colonel Lettow-Vorbeck, starting with a force of hardly 1,000 soldiers, successfully held off a British-led force which eventually included over 300,000 men in German Southeast Africa by a brilliant use of the guerrilla's strategy of trading space for time. But his forces were highly trained troops, not guerrilla bands, and his success as he himself intimated was due as much to the bungling of the thirty British generals who opposed him as to his own imaginative strategies.

Among the successful counterinsurgent leaders the proportion of successful generals is somewhat higher—due to the fact that it has been customary to send generals against guerrillas. However, the number of unsuccessful counterinsurgent generals is even higher: in the Indochina war, four senior French generals including a marshal were defeated in the end by the history teacher Giap. Probably the most successful counterinsurgent leader, as we have noted, was Magsaysay, an auto mechanic turned guerrilla, turned politician.

The unorthodoxy of guerrilla operations is an obstacle for a professional officer in whom orthodox methods have been inculcated during his entire career. However, as the Prussian-trained Lettow-Vorbeck demonstrated, this is not insurmountable provided the officer has the initiative and intelligence to forget his military school sand-table exercises.

Experience would thus seem to suggest that skills in orthodox military tactics and strategy are not an essential qualification for a guerrilla commander. On the contrary they would appear to be a liability. What then are the essential qualifications of the successful leader?

Obviously the candidate must have those characteristics that make a leader in any field: the charism to attract and hold a loyal following, organizational skills and above all ruthless determination in order to maintain discipline within the ranks and enforce discipline among the nonactive. For, in a sense, the guerrilla leader is far more than a commander. He is in fact the political governor of the areas where his writ runs, the administrator of the civil government, the police force and the judiciary to mete out punishment as he sees fit.

But beyond this there are two very special qualifications: a knowledge of the terrain and the ability to extract from it the maximum advantage.

By terrain I mean not merely the geographical aspects of the area, the rivers and roads, the mountains and the passes, but, more important, the social, economic and, above all, political features of the area. A successful guerrilla knows more than the hidden mountain trail unmarked on the military maps. He knows as well the political, religious and racial prejudices of the inhabitants. He knows the taboos, the local beliefs and superstitions, the particular grievances of particular strata and regions. He also knows the political personalities, their friendships and rivalries, their weaknesses and strengths. And naturally he knows their languages and patois.

But Mikhailovitch knew his terrain at least as well as Tito. Why then did he fail? We come to that final decisive characteristic which distinguishes the victorious from the defeated guerrilla: the ability to make the best use of the features of the social and political landscape to gain one's aims.

C. M. Woodhouse, the former head of the Allied mission to the Greek guerrillas during World War II, has divided guerrilla leaders into two categories he calls "the shaggy" and "the smooth."

"The shaggy" he defines as slow to co-ordinate their actions for a common purpose, easy-going, emotional rather than logical, inexact but well-meaning. In a word, the lumbering, often lovable Saint Bernard.

"The smooth" he describes as quick-witted, especially in assimilating Western techniques, logical rather than emotional, exact and competent and, above all, shrewd. The specifications conjure up the picture of a sleek, well-trained German police dog.

Woodhouse's archetypes are, as one would expect, for the shaggy Mikhailovitch, for the smooth Tito. (Tito's constant companion during the war years was a police dog taken from a German officer and whom he called "Tiger.")

For the terms shaggy and smooth one could perhaps substitute the politically naïve and the politically sophisticated. Whether he is shaggy or smooth determines how the guerrilla leader applies his essential knowledge to achieve his goals. Does he approach his goal with emotionally inspired faith that the righteousness of his cause will bring victory? Does he spurn guile and the unethical use of terror as unworthy of his crusade? Does he rate ardor above efficiency and ability among his subordinates?

Or does he shrewdly calculate his operations and coldbloodedly execute them without regard to ethical considerations? Does he put discipline and competence above friendship or humaneness? Does he demand training and learning through experience both of himself and his followers or rely instead on sheer bravery and determination?

Successful guerrillas almost invariably attach extreme importance to training and preparation. The Communist Party devotes the greatest effort to training its cadres. Grivas, who modeled his terrorist movement on Communism, spent months training his youthful followers before he launched his campaign in Cyprus. And the training consists not simply in studying guerrilla military tactics—how to shoot or lay an ambush—but in the manipulation of the political and economic and social forces that bear upon the outcome.

During his trial Mikhailovitch complained of his lack of experience: "The Partisans," he said wistfully, "had twenty years of experience of underground work and I had to take things as they were and improve on what I had."

It is sometimes said that rebels are born and that the born rebel will always find a cause for rebellion. Whether or not this is true in the free non-Communist world can be argued, but doubtless it is true that many a cause has failed for lack of an adequate leader.

But in the Communist empire leadership, like the cause, is not left to chance. Both are prepared in advance, ready to be launched when needed. Those inherent qualities of the natural leader which tend to attract followers and inspire loyalty are replaced in the Moscow-made leader by the structure of the Communist hierarchy and organization. For even Moscow seldom produces a leader with the natural talents of a Tito. Indeed, in view of the latter's success which led to his subsequent break with the Kremlin it is highly doubtful whether the Party's leaders would want any such talents among their agents in future.

The monolithic structure of the Party, with its strict internal disciplines and hierarchical prerogatives from the highest leader in the Kremlin to the lowest agent in the most distant land, assures that a guerrilla leader named by Moscow can count on the disciplined loyalty and obedience of his Communist subordinates whether his personality warrants such loyalty or not. For his authority derives not from his personal qualities but from his appointed position.

It is often supposed that Communist parties outside the empire are directed by high-cheeked Slavs, their shirttails flapping outside their trousers and their pockets bulging with revolvers or bombs. The contrary is ordinarily the case. Normally the Communist leaders are natives selected in their home areas after careful observation by the Party apparatus and thereafter brought to Moscow for their all-important training—the lack of which Mikhailovitch so regretted.

Wolfgang Leonhard in his fascinating book *Child of the Revolution** has described the education of the promising young men from foreign countries in the school system of the Communist Party.

Even before the recruit is enrolled in the Party in his native land he is impressed with the fact that he is being taken into a highly select, closely knit brotherhood, its rules not dissimilar to those of a religious order. Once enrolled the recruit's personal problems are subordinated to the major task of world revolution. Personal opinions and feelings are replaced by the Party line and directives from above.

For recruits from Southeastern Asia, training starts the moment their plane puts down at Tashkent airport, an elegant, lush, pompous structure designed to impress the visitor with the wealth and progress of the world's first Communist state which when the day comes they are going to copy and enjoy at home.

Subsequently, when they are put to work in the isolated schools of the Communist Party they are given little time and less opportunity to observe or reflect on the question whether life in the Soviet Union is as elegant and rich as the Tashkent airport led them to suppose.

Throughout their training, discipline, submission to higher

* Collins, London, 1957.

authority, is constantly drilled into them and when they return home they can be depended upon to inculcate the same discipline into their subordinates, down to the last guerrilla fighter.

Probably no less important than the inculcation of blind obedience is the extirpation of nationalist aspiration that might one day conflict with the "international" interests of the Communist empire. During Stalin's day, so great was his fear of such a conflict of interests that he all but destroyed the Communist International by liquidating its members whom he accused of "bourgeois nationalist tendencies."

Not all of the agents thus trained are returned to their native homes. Many are kept in Moscow to staff the foreign organization of the Party. Once this was the Communist International, abolished for diplomatic reasons by Stalin during World War II and subsequently replaced by the Cominform, later disbanded by Khrushchev in 1956 in the wake of the de-Stalinization program.

Today the "foreign office" of the Party, as distinct from the Foreign Office of the government, is an anonymous body about which little is known except that if precedent is any indication it is staffed largely by foreign Communists. Their function is to keep the Party apparatus informed of conditions in their native lands. The information they furnish is of two kinds: encyclopedic background knowledge of what I have referred to above as the "terrain"—political, economic and sociological. The other category is current information about the political scene: the personalities of leaders, their rivalries and alliances, their ambitions and prejudices and, of course, constant reports on the "temperature of the water" for whatever projects the Party may be considering in their areas.

These cadres, whether at home in their native lands or living in some obscure hostel in Moscow, are kept strictly separated from the formal Soviet diplomatic missions or the Foreign Office. Those in Moscow are in a sense governments-in-exile ready to be airlifted into their native lands and replace the governments to which Soviet diplomats have been accredited. For example, it was from the Moscow cadres of the Cominform that the governments of the Eastern European satellite countries were largely selected and flown into their native capitals almost as soon as the Soviet armies had conquered them. One of the few exceptions was Yugoslavia where, thanks to Tito's talents and the strength of his Partisan movement, a government already existed when the Soviet army arrived.

How effective is this system? Probably not as much as we have been led to believe. Since the war exiles from the European satellites have constantly warned that if the younger generation is not liberated before it completes its education under Communism it will be forever lost. Yet the Polish and Hungarian revolutions in 1956 indicate that young people are not as naïve or easily deceived as the teachers at the Party's educational institutions would like. Furthermore, the widespread antipathy for the Soviet system to be found among foreign students from underdeveloped countries in the universities of the Soviet Union and its satellites, as recently demonstrated by the riots of African students in Sofia, would lead one to suspect that students at the Party institutions are not completely blind to the realities of life in the Soviet Empire.

Nevertheless, it takes only a very few well-trained leaders to run a Communist liberation movement, and we must assume that in every country where the potential for such a movement exists there are also one or two ruthless, trained Communists biding their time and training their immediate staffs not only in the techniques of subversion and revolution but in the equally important aspects of discipline and devotion.

v The Development

MARSHAL DE LATTRE DE TASSIGNY, the newly arrived French Commander in Chief in Indochina, was puzzled and uneasy when on January 13, 1950, he read the message from the outposts of Vinh-Yen, thirty miles northwest of his headquarters at Hanoi. A strong force of Vietcong, the north Vietnamese Communist guerrillas, under General Giap, had attacked a small post called Bao-Chuc just beyond Vinh-Yen with a garrison of some fifty-odd Vietnamese and Senegalese soldiers. The attacking force appeared to be the Communist 308th Division, or a major part of it. Indications had been received that a further attack on Vinh-Yen itself was to be expected.

Only a few months before, Giap had overrun the French forts along the Chinese border and driven the French out of the northern portions of the country. Now that the Chinese Communists under Mao Tse-tung had defeated Chiang Kai-shek and stood on the border, it could be assumed that they would furnish Giap with the heavy weapons and supplies he so badly needed. Furthermore, by clearing the area north of Hanoi, Giap had acquired a safe base to train and reorganize his forces on conventional lines.

Giap's propaganda had been promising that Hanoi would be captured by mid-February. Did the attack on Bao-Chuc presage a general offensive? As the day wore on the news from Vinh-Yen grew more disturbing. A combat team sent to rescue the beleaguered troops in Bao-Chuc had been ambushed and suffered severe losses. The garrison of Bao-Chuc itself had been overwhelmed.

On January 14, the French forces had retreated into Vinh-Yen and were now virtually cut off from Hanoi by a three-mile stretch of undefended highway.

De Lattre de Tassigny decided the situation was serious enough for him personally to take command. With his light liaison plane he flew into Vinh-Yen. His first act was to order three crack battalions to be airlifted to Vinh-Yen from their post in South Vietnam a thousand miles away. Then he ordered another first-rate combat team to strike north from the direction of Hanoi with reserve ammunition for the combat team which had been ambushed.

A string of hills to the north on which the defense of Vinh-Yen depended had been overrun by Giap's guerrillas. Finally he ordered his re-enforcements to clear these hills at whatever cost.

By January 16, the French forces had to their surprise reoccupied the hills with practically no opposition. Once more Giap seemed to have vanished into thin air. Perhaps this was not the great offensive he had promised after all.

But in the late afternoon of that day, just as the sun was setting, French outposts reported that the Communist 308th Division was pouring down out of the mountains to the north in a general assault on the French hill positions. Now there was no doubt that this was the long-expected attack. De Lattre de Tassigny, who had returned to Hanoi, once more flew to Vinh-Yen, at the same time ordering every French fighter and transport plane that could carry a bomb into the attack to drop napalm on the attackers.

For many of the Vietcong guerrillas, this was their first experience with napalm. A Vietminh officer described its effect in his diary.

"All of a sudden," he wrote, "hell opens up in front of my eyes. Hell comes in form of large egg-shaped containers dropping from the first plane, followed by other eggs from the second and third planes. Immense sheets of flames, extending over hundreds of meters, it seems, strike terror in the ranks of my soldiers. This is napalm, the fire which falls from the skies.

"Another plane swoops down behind us and again drops a napalm bomb. The bomb falls close behind us and I feel its fiery breath touching my whole body. The men are now fleeing in all directions and I cannot hold them back."

As the officer tried to rally his men, he encountered another platoon commander.

"His eyes were wide with terror. 'What is this? The atomic bomb?'

" 'No, it is napalm,' the officer told him.

"The men continue to flee in all directions and I see a political commissar, pistol in hand trying desperately to regroup them.

"We can now hear clearly the yells of the enemy who is pursuing us. . . ."*

Thanks to the air attack, de Lattre de Tassigny roundly defeated Giap in that first Vietminh offensive, inflicting losses of over 6000 dead.

Nevertheless Giap struck twice more against the French to try to make good his promise to capture Hanoi, but both times he was defeated. Then he retired to take stock of the situation.

Giap was a careful student of Mao Tse-tung and fully accepted the latter's teaching that a successful guerrilla war must pass

* Quoted from Bernard B. Fall's *Street Without Joy.*

through three phases. In the first phase, the guerrillas are still too weak to attack the enemy and must constantly retreat before him. But as they retreat they gather strength while the enemy, extending his lines and penetrating deep into country already politically disaffected by the guerrillas, loses his *élan*.

At that point phase two begins when the guerrillas begin to worry the enemy, attacking his communications, harrying him when he pauses, ambushing his supply columns and capturing the weapons they need to form new guerrilla units. Finally comes the third phase when the enemy is too extended and weakened; and the guerrillas, re-enforced and better trained, move into the offensive, driving the enemy back and eventually defeating him. In this, the final phase, the guerrillas no longer operate in small bands but in large division-size units.

The trick is, however, as Mao warned, to recognize the moment in which to switch from one phase to another. If it is done too soon by an impatient commander, his units will be defeated in open battle against better-equipped, seasoned enemy troops as the Vietcong were defeated at Vinh-Yen with the aid of the napalm bombs. If it is postponed too long, one's own troops begin to get discouraged and the magic moment slips by forever.

Giap believed that the first phase of his war against the French had ended when he drove the occupiers out of their northern forts along the Chinese border in October 1950. He judged that the second phase had ended and the third begun when he made his massive attack at Vinh-Yen with the object of capturing Hanoi itself. Two subsequent unsuccessful attacks at Maokhe and Ninhbinh served only to underscore his mistaken timing.

Subsequently, when his strategy at the time was debated by the Communist Military Council, Giap was severely criticized and even threatened with removal. In the end he had to admit his error and resume the defensive for three long years until at Dien Bien Phu, his forces now twice as large and his firepower increased threefold, he was at last successful in defeating the French in a conventional siege and in reducing the French will to fight to the breaking point. In fact military writers point to the battle of Dien Bien Phu as the classic example of a third-phase operation which Giap had mistakenly attempted three years too soon at Vinh-Yen.

In practice, Mao Tse-tung's three phases are oversimplified descriptions of the successful development of a guerrilla movement. Mao's three-phase rule omits what is often the most decisive phase of all—the pre-combat, organizational or conspiratorial phase. During this preparatory stage, the guerrilla leader organizes his immediate staff and recruits and trains the nucleus of his fighting force. At the same time he tries to enlist the sympathy of the population in order to be sure of its support when combat operations start. He caches arms and supplies, prepares hide-outs and builds up a secret communications network whereby he can transmit orders and receive secret intelligence about the enemy when he later takes the field.

The reason for Mao's omission is clear when one considers the nature of the Communist structure itself. It is in fact a permanent conspiracy in a permanent pre-combat alert. Its leaders already appointed from above and their key cadres are always ready to take the field when the Kremlin feels it advantageous. The nucleus of the fighting force—the members of the Party—are in a permanent state of partial mobilization. The conspiratorial apparatus of the Party has a permanently established communications system and often a stockpile of weapons that may lie hidden for years awaiting the day.

When in 1948 the Malayan Communists were ordered to assume the offensive, they had a large stock of weapons supplied to them by the American OSS during the war with Japan four years earlier. The Huks too had weapons acquired from American sources in the fighting against the Japanese during the Philippine occupation.

Georg Grivas, the Cypriot terrorist, was anything but a Communist but for five years before he undertook his liberation campaign he carefully studied Communist methods of organization. After he landed on Cyprus he worked for six months in secrecy, organizing the pre-combat phase of his campaign of terror.

The success of this first pre-combat phase depends, of course, on absolute secrecy. The enemy's intelligence system and police force must not be aroused but lulled into a false sense of security until the security system of the guerrillas is sufficiently perfected and other preparations well on the way.

A police state enjoys a great advantage over a freer form of government against the guerrilla in this phase. Just as the Communist states have made full use of the guerrilla in their campaign against non-Communist countries, so too have they developed the most refined methods for preventing guerrilla action from being used against them.

Objectively, the Communist police state should provide the most fertile ground for antigovernment guerrillas. The political enslavement of the population, the economic sacrifices the Marxist system demands and the cultural, social and intellectual tyranny which are the hallmarks of Communist states are also among the surest ways of antagonizing the population and stimulating the fanatical hatred which the ideal guerrilla must have in order to take the risks and undergo the hardships of unconventional warfare.

But the Communist movement in modern times has also produced the most practical and ruthless experts in counterinsurgency. Well aware of the revolutionary opposition of their subjects (which they, of course, call counterrevolutionary), they have invariably maintained a system of police surveillance unexcelled in its vigilance.

When Mao Tse-tung writes that only "revolutionary" (read Communist) guerrilla wars can be successful and that "counterrevolutionary" (read anti-Communist) guerrilla wars are doomed to failure, he is in a sense right but for the wrong reasons. He asserts that counterrevolutionaries (anti-Communists) cannot win because they do not enjoy the support of the masses. The fact is, they seldom win because the vigilance of the Communist security police prevents their organizing and when they do rise, as in Warsaw and Budapest in 1956, without prior preparation or organized outside help, they are doomed by the superiority and ruthlessness of the Communist counterinsurgent police force.

When the Russian armies pushed the Germans out of the Soviet Union and advanced through hitherto non-Communist areas in eastern Europe, the Soviet political police were hard on the heels of the combat troops. While Communist propagandists endeavored to enlist the active support of the formerly discontented elements of the population, these police assiduously rounded up those who they knew would never support them— chiefly those with a material or intellectual stake in a freer society than that which they could expect under a Soviet system.

Since the proportion of the population favorable to them was usually small, it was occasionally necessary to establish a transitional government in which other parties were represented in order to obtain even a minimum of popular support. Thus in Austria a non-Communist Socialist was made head of the provisional government when the Red Army arrived in Vienna. However, in each of these governments, Soviet commissars made sure that the Minister of Interior and the police chiefs of the principle towns were either avowed or secret Party members. Their immediate function was to harass, render impotent and if necessary liquidate politicians and patriots whose loyalty they could not hope to win over by less drastic forms of persuasion. (In Austria the appearance of Western Allied troops prevented the process from reaching its logical conclusion.)

Thus from the very beginning the Communist leaders in the satellites made sure that any potential opposition would never have that first noncombatant phase of conspiratorial preparation essential to a successful guerrilla operation. In only one area were they unsuccessful—in the Soviet Union itself, specifically in the Ukraine and White Russia. Here, during the German occupation, nationalist elements had already passed through the conspiratorial phase and had become active guerrillas, initially against the German occupiers and, after they withdrew, against the Red Army.

This inability to nip conspiracy in the bud cost the Kremlin dearly, and for several years after the defeat of Germany, nationalist bands of Ukrainian and White Russian guerrillas continued to wage active war against the Soviet internal security forces. Hiding out in swamps and forests of western Russia these bands often enjoying the clandestine support of the population managed to subsist and to carry out isolated marauding raids and political assassinations. However, in the end, deprived of outside support which prevented their growth into larger units capable of resisting Soviet conventional forces, they were finally worn down and suppressed.

For non-Communist systems of government the prevention of guerrilla wars during the initial conspiratorial phase poses greater problems than for Communist states. In the first place, non-Communist police systems are seldom so vast or so thorough as those of the Communists. Restricted not only by constitutional guarantees of freedom, such as freedom of assembly and habeas corpus, they are legally deprived of many of the Communist police's most effective weapons. Furthermore, restrained by popular opposition to the methods of torture and persecution, they can seldom be as ruthless in wiping out potential centers of opposition which might develop into guerrilla conspiracies.

The failure of the British authorities in Cyprus to take action against Colonel Grivas in the initial phase of his terrorist campaign, when he was most vulnerable, is a case in point. The constitutional right of habeas corpus in Magsaysay's fight against the

Huks (until he modified it) exemplifies the type of obstacle constitutional government imposes on even the most vigorous police surveillance in the pre-combat, conspiratorial phase of a guerrilla operation whether it be Communist or Fascist inspired.

The initial combat phase, which Mao calls the first phase, is hardly less crucial for a guerrilla movement. During this stage of combat, it is faced by superior police and army forces of the enemy and is forced to exchange space for time while it consolidates its own forces, arms them with weapons captured or stolen from the enemy or imported from its foreign allies, and seeks to draw the superior enemy into areas rendered hostile to him by the guerrilla's propaganda. Meantime, by constant hit-and-run raids on the enemy's lines of communication, it harries wherever it can without risking losses.

Eventually a sort of equilibrium is reached when further advance for the enemy is too costly while the guerrilla band itself is too weak to force it to retreat. Only then can the guerrilla force maintain and be assured of relative security in bases into which the enemy dares not intrude except for temporary raiding expeditions. In these bases, the guerrillas can not only establish rest and training camps but can set up more-or-less-permanent supply centers, repair shops for captured weapons and even arsenals where new weapons can be forged.

But until this point is reached, the guerrilla is still highly vulnerable. His troops tend to become demoralized with constant retreat, faced by troops superior in numbers, training and equipment. The civilian supports, too, begin to doubt the ability of the irregulars to achieve eventual success and are tempted to side with the pursuing counterinsurgent forces.

But the latter are also vulnerable. Usually commanded by professional officers, the counterinsurgent tends to underrate his adversary, pursuing at leisure and according the rules of the book. Loath to take the irregulars seriously, at first, the counterinsurgent authorities likewise almost invariably assign inadequate forces and matériel to their liquidation. As if intentionally making things more difficult for themselves, they tend to treat the civilian population which has harbored the guerrillas as traitors and alienate themselves even more from this source of support— as we have noted in the pre-Magsaysay period of the Huk rebellion. Only when the counterinsurgent finds himself unable by orthodox methods to run down the insurgents does he begin to take his task seriously. But by then it is often too late, as the French discovered when they were driven from the border areas in the north of Indochina.

Now the counterinsurgent has no alternative but to gird himself for the "protracted war" which as Mao predicts is practically inevitable. Emerging at will from its safe bases, the insurgent force is in a position to strike where and when it wants at enemy convoys, patrols and isolated strong points. Though it is still unable to face the enemy in open combat or to defend any important position against a major assault it can, as Mao says, harass the enemy like "innumerable gnats which by biting a giant in front and in the rear, ultimately exhaust him."

Carefully planning their operations so that they never risk major defeat, the guerrillas gradually force the counterinsurgents to the defensive while they, on the other hand, constantly consolidate their forces, increasing the size of their units from tiny bands to battalions capable of attacking ever larger enemy concentrations. Now every successful strike raises the guerrilla morale, restores the confidence of the civilian population and its foreign allies in its eventual success and reduces the counterinsurgent force to a state of ebbing hope of ever being able to exterminate the innumerable gnats which harass it at every unexpected moment.

Finally comes the third stage—that moment when the insurgents are able to hold an area against any attack and in it reorganize their forces into a conventional army. Provided they are able at this stage to acquire the arms and equipment such an army needs, they are ready to challenge the enemy in face-to-face battle. Now conventional warfare replaces irregular combat and the outcome will depend on the comparative military strength and ability and will to win of the two adversaries.

Although this three-phase formula of Mao Tse-tung's led to the defeat of Chiang Kai-shek, it is by no means an invincible strategy or even the only successful strategy of guerrilla war. As we have already intimated, it depends largely on the initial short-sightedness of the counterinsurgent in the pre-combat stage and on his slothful counteraction in the early combat phases.

Furthermore, the timing of each phase is crucial. If, as in the Bay of Pigs operation, the combat phase is begun before adequate preparations have been made, defeat is practically inevitable. Or, if an over-zealous guerrilla leader moves from the second, harassing phase into conventional-type warfare, as Giap did at Vinh-Yen, the whole movement can be jeopardized.

Finally, as in every form of warfare, military victory is by no means synonymous with success. The Western Allies, together with the Soviet Union, won World War II but they did not achieve their ultimate political aim of a peaceful democratic Europe, as expressed in the Atlantic Charter.

The Vietcong Communists, on the other hand, achieved their political aim without a decisive military victory. The French defeat at Dien Bien Phu, while fatal to the French will to resist, was by no means militarily decisive, for the French troops involved comprised only a small fraction of the French forces in Indochina at the time.

Clausewitz, as we have noted, pointed out that war can be and frequently is terminated short of military destruction or defeat of the enemy. When the political aim of the enemy involves a comparatively smaller sacrifice than the probable outlay required to defeat him, the will to resist him will be correspondingly smaller. In the case of the Indochinese war, the prospect of eventually defeating the Vietcong was so dim after Dien Bien Phu, and the probable outlay in lives and funds so great, that the French political leaders in Paris preferred to sue for peace.

In Castro's rebellion against Batista, the will to resist of Batista's forces was so low and the inner strength of the regime so decayed that it collapsed before Castro even entered the third or final phase of the struggle.

Frequently in countries where political power is concentrated in a thin stratum of society, as in many Latin American countries, only the pre-combat, conspiratorial phase is necessary before the government is overthrown by a *coup d'état*. Only when significant numbers of the population feel themselves involved in the struggle does the rebellion pass to the protracted combat phase.

vi The Base

Captain George Nikitas was an old soldier with considerable fighting experience. Though he liked his profession he definitely did not like his present assignment. Fighting against one's own compatriots was never pleasant, even though his enemies were Communists and as such he considered them traitors to the royal government in Athens. Besides, counterguerrilla operations had little in common with the regular warfare for which he had been trained. The enemy seldom showed themselves and then only in small groups. They almost never fought like regulars but hid behind rocks and in gullies in the desolate mountains of Greek Macedonia and sniped at the Captain's patrols. When he attacked with anything like equal strength they did not hold their ground and permit him to show his skill in deploying his troops, placing his mountain artillery or maneuvering as one did on an ordinary battlefield. Instead they simply fled, melting into the rugged landscape and waiting for another chance to shoot when he least expected it.

And now a special circumstance made his task even more difficult and disagreeable. Operating within sight of the Yugoslav
border, all the guerrillas had to do if they were hard pressed was
to slip across the frontier where the Communist government of
Marshal Tito welcomed them and gave them refuge. Captain
Nikitas, on the other hand, was under strict orders not to shoot
across the border under any circumstances or even to operate
within a thousand yards of it. The latter rule he occasionally vio-
lated but the no-shooting order, he realized, was another matter
as it might provoke Tito's army to counterattack, and because of
its strength it could sweep aside the entire Greek National Army
and march straight into Athens itself.

This guerrilla privilege of taking refuge across the border was,
the Captain thought, not just unfair, unsporting and against all
the rules of neutrality. It made it almost impossible to round up
the Communist "bandits," as they were called by the Greeks.

For months soldiers of the Greek National Army had been
slowly creeping northward, pushing the Communist bands ahead
of them. Now as they approached the border, this final operation
had been designated a "mopping-up." But as Captain Nikitas was
all too well aware, while they had swept northward, dozens of
small guerrilla bands had slipped back south through the lines and
were soon re-established in mountain strongholds in the rear.

Nevertheless a large band of four or five hundred were, he
knew, still somewhere ahead between him and the Yugoslav
frontier. Intelligence reports indicated that they had set up a
more or less permanent headquarters and camp a mile or two
south of the border in Greek territory. If only he could slip his
forces between the camp and the Yugoslav haven in the north,
then in conjunction with another column moving up east of him
it might be possible to encircle the band and annihilate it.

That at least was the strategy. But the chances for success were
slight, for the guerrillas had patrols operating all about him. Ear-

lier in the day as he had advanced from Mouries, a village now ten miles to the south, his column had been attacked by a small group of guerrillas, but as soon as he had turned his Bren gun on them they had fled. He had managed to cut off from the border one small group on his right flank but it had slipped south, across his rear, and the last he had seen of the seven or eight men in it they were scrambling down a gully on the other side of which lay that accursed frontier. The rest of the band he had watched crossing the border at Ana Kouka on his left front.

Around four o'clock, when the sun was low on the horizon, his advance guard reported another band of guerrillas seeking refuge in a small forest below him on his right front. Probably, he concluded, this was the site of the headquarters camp. Carefully he made his dispositions to attack and try to cut the force off from the border but hardly had he trained his guns on the wood when he heard heavy fire coming from his left rear.

At first the bullets flew high overhead and inflicted no damage but soon the bandit riflemen had the range and his column was forced to take cover among the rocks. One of his platoon leaders climbed to the peak of a hill and came back to report that the fire was coming from a Yugoslav frontier post a few hundred yards away. Just to make sure, Captain Nikitas climbed the peak himself and through his binoculars confirmed the fact that the fire was indeed coming from Yugoslav territory. Doubtless it was the group of bandits whom he had seen crossing over at Ana Kouka who had crept up behind him, sheltered by the Yugoslav frontier, and were now pinning him down to prevent his attacking the forest below. His first instinct was to return the fire. He could always claim later that he did not know where the Yugoslav border was. But then, as though reading his thoughts, the Yugoslavs raised a flag over the frontier post.

As night fell, the firing ceased, but by now it was too late to attack the guerrillas for his presence was known and to attempt a surprise thrust in the darkness against a well-posted camp was futile.

But next day at first light he moved his column forward. The firing from his rear had not resumed and he made his way unopposed into the forest. There, exactly as he had expected, he found a full-fledged camp: some thirty wooden huts with double rows of bunks, a small hospital and the remains of a field arsenal where the guerrillas had repaired their weapons. Leading from the camp was a trail going straight north to the border. It was so well trodden, he later testified, that it looked like a village street.

Glowing embers in the camp fires and the skins of freshly butchered sheep still wet with blood were proof that the camp had been abandoned during the night. There was no doubt now that the fire from the Yugoslav outpost the day before had been directed to pinning him down while the evacuation got under way. Once again the "mopping-up" had failed.

Some time later, Nationalist troops captured a guerrilla who testified before the United Nations Commission sent to investigate Greek charges of Yugoslav aid to the guerrillas that he had been among the five hundred bandits at the camp Captain Nikitas had threatened. During the late afternoon as Captain Nikitas approached, the prisoner Mikhailides, who commanded a mortar detachment, had been ordered back to camp. Thence his men had been taken to the border where they were met by Yugoslav soldiers and guided to a camp three miles inside Yugoslav territory. There they had been ordered to lay down their arms and cover them with branches as camouflage from Greek planes. A detachment of Yugoslav soldiers had guarded the weapons until, after a few days of rest, the Greek guerrillas had gone back to Greek territory.

At first glance it seems strange that the Yugoslavs insisted on disarming their fellow Communists but one must remember that at that time Tito was not in full command of his own country where anti-Communist bands still roamed the country. Tito's border guards were evidently taking no chances that the anti-Communist Greeks might infiltrate armed bands into his territory in the guise of Communist guerrillas.

Before the outbreak of World War II the Greek Communist Party had few members and practically no influence. However, during the Italian and German occupation, it had made the most of the intensely nationalistic spirit of the Greek people to organize a National Liberation Front (EAM) and a National Liberation Army (ELAS) both of them under clandestine Communist control. During the occupation the Allies, operating presumably on Churchill's criterion—who's-killing-the-most-Germans?—gave them considerable assistance by dropping arms to the ELAS. Later, as Hitler's divisions withdrew northward, the Germans bought freedom from ELAS harassment by giving it the weapons they no longer could take with them.

In February 1945, two months after liberation, a bloody clash in the Athens area between the British Army and the Greek Nationalists on the one hand and the Communists on the other was finally halted with a truce which lasted for two years. During that period the Communist organization remained quiet but clandestinely was active organizing and training military cadres. At the same time it organized a highly efficient "self-defense" organization among the nonactive, civilian population and charged it with gathering intelligence, funds, recruits and food for the active guerrillas. Early in 1946 small fighting units took to the hills where they set up strongpoints supported by the clandestine "self-defense" units in the villages.

From the beginning the guerrillas enjoyed the open sympathy and support of the neighboring satellite regimes, chiefly Yugoslavia, and to a less active degree Albania and Bulgaria. From transmitters across the border a steady flood of broadcasts flooded the Greek ether with Communist political propaganda. Arms, ammunition and other supplies flowed equally freely across the frontiers. Not only could Communist guerrilla bands fleeing from government troops seek haven beyond the border but in Bulkes, a town in southern Yugoslavia, a military school was set up to train soldiers and officers for the Communist guerrilla forces in Greece.

The Greek National Army, commanded by elderly generals untrained in unconventional warfare, fruitlessly attempted to drive the Communists out of their strongholds, corner them and force them to battle. The guerrillas, however, skillfully avoided engagements with superior forces but constantly attacked small undefended or lightly defended villages and towns where they murdered whatever Nationalist leaders they could find, abducted the young men and looted what supplies they needed. Inevitably the politicians in Athens demanded that the army and constabulary station adequate forces in provincial towns to protect their constituencies, thus dissipating the army's strength and making any effective offensive against the guerrillas still less possible.

From 1947 on each spring for three years the National Army went into action and combed the country from south to north, trying to bottle up the guerrillas. But each winter when the army returned to barracks the Communists filtered back into the mountain strongholds from which they had been driven.

Meantime the British abdicated their position as principle protectors of the Greek government and were replaced by the Americans who under the Truman Doctrine began furnishing economic and military aid in substanial quantities. Finally, in January 1949, General Papagos, a wartime hero, was once more given command of the army. He demanded and was granted freedom from the political interference which had hobbled his predecessors. Together with the American command he worked out a systematic plan of campaign which was promptly put into operation. Once more a sweep from the south was undertaken, but instead of the leisurely pace of previous campaigns Papagos drove his troops in relentless pursuit of every guerrilla band he located. Furthermore, as villages were liberated from Communist control, homeguards were organized to prevent their return and the population was subjected to massive anti-Communist indoctrination to prevent what Papagos called "reinfection."

As the campaign progressed, Papagos was blessed with two strokes of good fortune. The first was a shift in Communist guerrilla strategy. The brilliant Communist guerrilla leader Markos Vafiades was relieved of command and his place taken by the political leader of the Communist Party, Nicolas Zachariades. Shortly thereafter Zachariades scrapped Vafiades' practice of keeping his forces divided into small units which, while avoiding head-on clashes with the regular troops, constantly harassed them and the anti-Communist village homeguard. Instead Zachariades began forming large brigades with which he attempted to hold an area of Greek territory against assaults by government troops.

Thus Zachariades attempted to leap directly from the defensive tactics of Mao's first phase into the third or final phase of conventional warfare. The change was doubtless dictated by political considerations. If he could hold permanently a part of Greek territory and establish on it a de facto Communist government he would not only score a great propaganda victory but also he could claim official recognition from the surrounding Communist regimes in Albania, Yugoslavia and Bulgaria and demand from them the additional heavy equipment necessary to convert his guerrilla bands into a conventional army.

The area he chose to hold was the mountainous region around Grammos and Vitsi on the Greek-Yugoslav-Albanian border. Once before the guerrillas had taken and fortified this territory but had been driven out by the regular Greek army. The second attempt was no more successful. And this time it was accompanied by another blow which proved fatal—the withdrawal of Yugoslav support.

In 1948 Tito had defied Stalin and broken away from the Communist empire ruled by the Kremlin. At the time of the break he pledged continued support for Markos' forces but early in 1949, apparently disturbed by a political move sponsored by Moscow to create a "Greater Macedonia" under Bulgarian rule which would include Yugoslav territory, he first reduced his aid to the Greek Communists and then in July 1949 closed his frontiers to their forces altogether. No longer could guerrilla bands seek sanctuary behind his border as they had in the days when Captain Nikitas was pursuing them through the mountains. No longer could recruits be sent to Bulkes for training and no longer could they rely on a steady supply of food and weapons from the north.

Within a matter of weeks, Greek National troops had once more recaptured Grammos and Vitsi. Only a few hungry, battered bands of Communist guerrillas fought for survival in the Greek mountains. Finally the "Free Greek Government," driven back into Albania, proclaimed an end to hostilities, and the guerrilla war which had dragged on for more than three long years was brought to an end.

The appointment of the vigorous and able Field Marshal Papagos and the sacking of the brilliant guerrilla leader Markos had much to do with the final outcome but the closing of the Yugoslav sanctuary was in the end the decisive factor in the Greek government's victory.

In conventional warfare, the base is the heart of all military operations. In pre-Napoleonic days, before large armies were deployed, it might even have been a walled castle where supplies were assembled and refuge given both to the passive civilian

population and the army in times of need. It might have been
a capital city or a communications center where the supplies
were gathered. Nowadays it might be a whole country or segment of a country containing the munitions factories and agricultural areas which produce the weapons and food to support
the army.

The object of the enemy was generally to capture the base areas
or, failing that, to cut off the arteries of supply leading from it
to the troops in the field. When a general sallied forth on an
offensive operation, he made sure with every mile he advanced
that his supply lines were safe from interdiction by the enemy,
lest he be cut off and rendered helpless by lack of munitions.
Though even in modern days a small regular force can live off
the land for a time, gathering food from the countryside by
foraging parties, rarely can it subsist for long if deprived of
its source of ammunition, weapons and recruits to replace
casualties.

At first glance it would seem that the essential difference between guerrilla bands and regular forces is that the guerrillas
are independent of bases. They carry their weapons and rations
with them and renew their supplies of munitions by attacking the
enemy supply dumps. They live off the country, either pillaging
for food or getting it from a friendly population. Their refuge is
usually the jungle or the desert or inaccessible mountains. But
such refuge is only adequate if the enemy does not pursue
them.

In World War I, Lawrence's Arab bands were seldom pursued by the Turks, who maintained a static defense along the
railroads and in large towns. Consequently, after every major
sortie the Arab forces were able to recuperate, re-form and rest in
small oases deep in the desert. Similarly, in the first stages of the
Greek Civil War the Communists could escape to the mountains
and hole up in small villages so long as the Greek army stuck to

the big towns and moved only on main roads. Mao had been able to resist a far more powerful Japanese army by retreat and dispersal deep in the Chinese hinterland.

But sooner or later professional soldiers in counterinsurgent operations realize that they must relentlessly pursue every band and be prepared to penetrate the most inhospitable terrain in that pursuit. And sooner or later, the guerrilla must stop running if only to catch his breath. Though small bands and individuals can elude pursuit by hiding, this too becomes impossible as the size of the guerrilla force grows.

Then too a larger food supply is needed, which means a larger productive area from which to buy, beg or steal. Bases are also essential for training of new recruits to swell the guerrilla force. The wounded pose a special problem. Few guerrillas will fight courageously for long if they know that the slightest incapacity means they must be abandoned to the enemy and presumably to a firing squad. On the other hand if they are assured of a base area where they can be treated and convalesce, they will run the risks of combat with considerably more courage and daring.

As Mao Tse-tung takes care to warn, an area where the guerrilla operates and even controls movement by night but whence he must flee when the enemy appears is not a base area. To be of any use a base area need not be permanent but it must be tenable for a continuous period of time. In the Greek Civil War, the Communists established seasonal bases in the wintertime. In Vietnam today, the guerrillas frequently retire to safe jungle areas in the monsoon period when pursuit is almost impossible.

As Lawrence discovered, the "vast empty desert" furnished ideal base areas. The Russian Partisans in World War II found the swamps and huge forest areas of White Russia and the Ukraine havens from pursuing German counterguerrilla forces. Mao Tse-tung points out that mountain areas are probably the safest terrain for permanent bases. Tito in the mountains of

Montenegro and Castro in the Escambray Mountains came to the same conclusion.

Mao also pointed out that areas crisscrossed by rivers or canals are excellent for guerrilla bases since the waterways provide ideal paths for assembly in preparation for a raid and for dispersal thereafter and they leave no telltale tracks. By holding a base along an important water route, guerrillas can also deny its use to the enemy by relatively easy raids.

Flat open country if heavily settled, even if the population is friendly, is not, Mao says, suitable for bases. The frequency of roads, the lack of cover and the facilities for moving large regular forces in such areas deprive the guerrillas of their greatest advantages—greater mobility and concealment.

Mao also maintains that in small countries such as Belgium guerrilla operations are not possible. Other military leaders have come to the belief that with the exception of a few relatively large forest or swamp areas, western Europe is completely unsuited to guerrilla warfare. However, considerable evidence indicates that highly effective guerrilla operations can be carried out —though by very small units—in thickly populated areas. (We shall return to this important question in another chapter.)

Wherever the base is established an indispensable condition must prevail: the local population must be "friendly." That is, a substantial segment of it must be willing to work actively for the guerrillas, collecting food, providing transportation and furnishing such facilities as tool shops and hospital care. The rest of the population, though inactive, must be reliable enough to furnish information on enemy movements beyond the periphery of the base or at least to deny information to the enemy as to the disposition of the guerrillas.

For all their theorizing on guerrilla wars, Communist writers such as Mao and Che Guevara are notably silent about the best, if not indeed indispensable, base area for every successful guerrilla movement—a friendly foreign territory contiguous to or easily accessible from the guerrilla area. Their reason is obvious— to maintain the myth of independent, indigenous "liberation wars" and to disguise the fact that most of them are organized, led and supplied by established Communist governments.

In conventional war, the laws of neutrality require that a neutral nation must not only refrain from outright military assistance to belligerents in a war but must intern for the duration all belligerent troops seeking refuge within its borders. If it gives aid to one side and permits one belligerent to seek temporary asylum, it automatically loses its neutral status and becomes a belligerent itself.

In World War I, the aid rendered to the French and British by the United States laid it open to violating the laws of neutrality and this aid (though not strictly military) was used by the Germans as a pretext for attacking American shipping. When the laws of neutrality first took form, military aid was relatively easy to define as munitions of war. However, as warfare became more all-embracing, all forms of aid, including food, became weapons and thus fell under the interdiction of neutrality laws. In the case of Mao Tse-tung, the aid he received from the Soviet Union was relatively small except in the final phase of his struggle against Chiang Kai-shek after the elimination of the Japanese. At that point the Soviet armies which occupied Manchuria when the Japanese withdrew placed at the disposal of Mao's guerrillas practically all the munitions, weapons and equipment captured from the Japanese. With these weapons Mao managed to equip large units that eventually defeated Chiang.

In the case of Castro, the base of his operations was, curiously enough, the United States. From agents, covert and open, he managed not only to recruit reinforcements from anti-Batista exiles but also to get funds and even the latest weapons from private American manufacturers to equip his units in the mountains.

In fact, in some instances he was able to acquire weapons so modern that they had not even been widely issued to American troops.

However, for Castro the American base was far from satisfactory. The neutrality of the United States prevented open American assistance and required Castro's agents to work clandestinely. American assistance smacking of "Yankee imperialism" was also a political liability.

Furthermore, the American base could not be used as a safe haven for tired or wounded troops, or as a training area for recruits. Lacking these essential facilities, it is doubtful whether Castro could ever have won had not the Batista regime been so weakened by internal decay and corruption that it could not command the loyalty of its own officers, to say nothing of its soldiers.

With the possible exception of the Castro movement in this respect, few indigenous guerrilla wars have been successfully fought to a conclusion without foreign aid. Certainly no Communist-inspired civil war has succeeded without Communist support. The artillery Mao furnished Ho Chi Minh was largely responsible for the fall of Dien Bien Phu, which in turn persuaded France to give up the struggle for Indochina. The Communist Huks, as we have seen, were eliminated by isolation as were the Communist guerrillas in Malaya. Denied a safe haven in Yugoslavia, the Greek Communist guerrillas collapsed in a matter of weeks.

Until recent times, to provide a safe haven it was necessary for the friendly "neutral" to have a common frontier with the guerrilla area or at least unopposed access by land routes such as Laos provides for the Vietcong against South Vietnam. However, the development of aviation, especially the helicopter and the techniques of parachuting, has made it possible to provide guerrillas not only with food and weapons but also with facilities for evacuating wounded and training areas for recruits from far-off noncontiguous sources.

In the last two years of World War II, Tito's Partisans maintained to all intents and purposes a base in Bari, Italy, to which wounded were flown from Yugoslavia and whence a supply mission sent equipment and weapons which in the final phases of the war against Germany included even tanks, trucks and heavy artillery. Toward the end of the war the Balkan Air Force (operated by the British) dropped scores of planeloads of supplies to the Partisan forces every night. With these weapons Tito was able in the end to organize his forces along conventional lines, face the Germans in open combat and thus, long afterward, to claim that his own indigenous forces and not the Soviet army had liberated Yugoslavia.

Even before the war had ended, however, Tito and his colleagues tended to minimize in their public statements the extent of the aid they had received from the West. Celebrating the capture of Belgrade at a banquet at which this writer was present, one of Tito's principal aides proposed a toast to the Soviet Union which "had provided the rifles for the creation of the Yugoslav Partisan forces." At that time the great majority of rifles in Partisan hands were made in America or captured from the Italian and German enemy.

During World War II, the Soviet Union was not equipped to furnish long-range aid to Partisan forces far beyond the borders of Russia. Nor had the Red Army developed the technical skills to carry out such operations. However, there is considerable evidence that these deficiencies have largely been overcome as the supply of the Communist-led Pathet Lao forces indicates.

Until recently, the Kremlin leaders shied away from supporting "liberation wars" in countries not contiguous to or easily accessible from the Communist empire. However, it would be folly to assume that, provided other factors are favorable, the Communist leadership would hesitate to instigate and provide the essential foreign base by air for "liberation movements" as far away as Africa or even South America.

Theoretically, a base area of sufficient size can produce or furnish the necessary food supplies, uniforms and equipment, including the less sophisticated weapons such as rifles, to equip a conventional force entering Mao's third phase. In practice, however, a foreign base of supplies is today almost essential before a guerrilla force can be converted into a regular army adequately armed with tanks, heavy artillery and intricate communications equipment. As we have noted above, even Mao, though he never acknowledged the fact, received much of his heavy equipment from the Japanese armies captured at the war's end by the Soviet Army.

This dependence on foreign sources introduces one of the most delicate problems posed by guerrilla movements today. For acceptance of foreign arms does not merely expose the guerrilla to the charge of being a puppet of a foreign regime. It does, in fact, open him to external pressures to compromise his original political aims.

Despite the relative ease with which aid to a guerrilla movement can be rendered clandestinely and without open violation of the laws of neutrality, the costs in money and material alone, not to mention the loss of prestige in the event of failure, make it a risky investment at best. In wartime, when prestige is of less concern, the decision to back a resistance movement is often made from purely military considerations—as we have noted in the case of Tito. But as this case also illustrates, overriding military considerations of the moment often conflict with the long-range political aims for which the war is being fought. Had Mikhailovitch received the same massive support that eventually went to Tito and used it as Tito did, the current picture in the Balkans might be considerably different and more favorable to the very countries which gave Tito support in his most critical hour.

In peacetime, the variety of motives for supporting a popular uprising vary greatly but one could perhaps group them under the single heading of creating a friendly government or replacing an unfriendly one. The American efforts successful in Guatemala and unsuccessful in the Bay of Pigs fall into the latter category. The Communist uprisings in Greece, Burma, Malaya and Vietnam obviously fall into the first category.

Contrary to general belief, the Soviet government has by no means supported all "revolutionary" movements against a "capitalist" regime. Indeed Stalin's Communist opponents have charged since his death that he was basically opposed to revolutions abroad. This is perhaps an exaggeration. Actually he appeared to favor most popular Communist uprisings *provided they did not interfere with his long-range foreign policy and provided they were thoroughly under his control.*

The Spanish Revolution illustrates his attitude. For some time after Franco revolted against the Socialist Spanish regime, Stalin hesitated to come to the latter's aid, fearful that it might embroil him in a conflict with the western European powers which he could at the time scarcely afford. But then he changed his mind and ordered all-out support of the Loyalists. At the same time he instructed his political police to assure that the leadership of the Loyalists was fully under his control and that those who opposed him were summarily liquidated.

But as Milovan Djilas has pointed out, Stalin was always ready to leave revolutions in the lurch when they slipped from his grasp. This is precisely what he did when the Spanish Loyalists faltered. Stalin's attitude toward Mao Tse-tung at critical moments and even in the early stages toward Tito indicated anything but all-out support.

Djilas is of the opinion that "even today there is not any essential change in this respect in the policy of the Soviet [Khrushchev] government."

We have already examined how the Kremlin attempts to assure

its control over popular Communist uprisings through its carefully schooled agents. The problem for non-Communist governments is more difficult since they are ill prepared to select, train and launch an agent as the head of a popular uprising. The question for them is whether, if they support a given leader, they can exert a telling influence on him in the long range. Obviously when a movement is in dire need of arms and equipment, it can usually be constrained to follow the advice of those who are prepared to support it. But once launched on the road to victory, will it remain compliant?

Is the leadership "shaggy" or "smooth"? Is it idealistic, inefficient but benevolent? If so, is it capable of being made effective by sound advice and expert instruction? If it is smooth, is it sincerely attached to the aims it professes? If it is openly Communist can it be weaned, as some thought of Tito, from its Moscow loyalties by timely aid and comfort in the hour of adversity? If it is avowedly anti-Communist, is it secure against penetration and subversion?

Accurate answers to such questions about guerrilla movements are even more difficult to obtain than about the most obscure but less militant movements. Whether it be Mao Tse-tung hidden away in the depths of inner China, or Tito in a cave in Bosnia or Mikhailovitch in the forests of southern Serbia, the very nature of their business makes them anything but accessible. Even when observers are dropped into their camps, the secrecy of the operations makes it relatively simple to prevent the over-curious foreigner from examining the movement too closely. Furthermore, while he is a guest in their camp, he is completely at their mercy. He is indebted to them for his safety, his comfort and, in the last analysis, for his safe return to his base. Under such circumstances objectivity is put under considerable strain.

It is hardly a wonder that Mao Tse-tung was so often described as an agrarian reformer, Tito as a progressive Yugoslav Left-wing nationalist "weanable" from his attachment to Moscow, or Castro and his followers as idealistic democratic reformers.

Woodhouse, who classified guerrilla leaders as "shaggy" or "smooth," describes the British liaison officers sent to resistance movements in Europe as either amateurs or professionals: happy-go-lucky idealists and adventurers on one hand and serious, politically experienced men, carefully trained in the techniques of irregular warfare on the other.

Americans sent by the OSS on similar missions fell roughly into the same categories: officers recruited from civilian life who sought dangerous and romantic assignments for which they often had few qualifications but courage, and a handful of politically trained men who had some background in the languages and the political intricacies of Europe and had acquired a smattering of the techniques of guerrilla operations, often from their British allies.

However, among the American liaison staffs was a third category of first- or second-generation Americans whose families had emigrated from the guerrilla area and who therefore had an invaluable knowledge of the local languages and customs and histories. This last category had one drawback: they almost inevitably reidentified themselves with the milieux from which their families had originally come, with all the prejudices, emotional reactions, jealousies and rivalries as well as political viewpoints of their parents. Some came from sturdy, conservative peasant stock; others from radical, occasionally Communist-inclined intellectuals; and still others from moderate merchant families. Few who had retained their knowledge of their original language had become sufficiently integrated Americans to be able to observe and report with the objectivity essential for a wise policy decision on the question of supporting the various resistance groups.

But the greatest handicap in all categories was the lack of experience in the political or ideological in-fighting which split the various resistance movements. Few were even temperamentally suited to the ruthless, conspiratorial methods of their competitors schooled in the Communist Party organization in the Soviet Union.

Though this lack of adequately trained personnel was a serious, sometimes fatal, handicap in the more sophisticated struggles in Europe or even China, it was less important in other areas where the lines were drawn by simpler criteria and where, as in Southeast Asia, the political nuances of democratic versus dictatorial systems were less developed. In these areas, at least in the wartime phase, the population divided itself into antis, pros or neutrals vis-à-vis the Japanese. Only after the war did the finer ideological distinctions in the various guerrilla movements come to the surface.

Whether this deficiency in adequately trained personnel can be remedied, and by what means, in a non-Communist country is a matter that must be postponed until we examine those other peculiarities and techniques of modern guerrilla movements which distinguish them from conventional wars.

VII Isolation

Major John was not the type of man to call his assignment to the village of Kampong Jalong in the Malay jungle a challenge. Yet for the big, rawboned Australian infantryman that was precisely what it was, and when his superiors had selected him for the job, they had been guided largely by his sound political sense and his flare for getting along with people.

The village itself, devoid of all charm, was a dreary compound of newly built row houses surrounded by a high barricade just on the outskirts of an old trading town on the bank of the Siput River in Central Malaya. Built to house some fifteen hundred Chinese, Malays and Indians who had previously dwelt in small scattered communities in the vicinity, it had all the characteristics of a refugee camp. Like six or seven hundred thousand other jungle dwellers, they had been rounded up from their settlements and individual squatter huts in the jungle in pre-dawn raids by British and Australian soldiers and taken by truck to the new compound where they were given materials to build their new homes.

The high barbed-wire fence which surrounded the site had only two gates—one opening onto the old town by the river, the other opening onto the rubber plantations to the west. Both the gates and the fence itself were constantly guarded by soldiers and native homeguards—"for the protection of the villagers," the authorities said. But the villagers knew better. Actually the fence was to cut them off from their friends and relatives who had joined the Communist guerrillas in the jungle that surrounded the village and the plantations where most of them worked.

Although the British authorities and the native Malay government officials called the guerrillas bandits, most of the villagers had looked upon them as heroes. During World War II, when the Japanese had overrun the Malay Peninsula, they had taken to the jungle where they had been organized and trained by Communist Party men. American and British officers had fought with them against the Japanese occupiers, and for a brief period after the Japanese surrendered, they had enjoyed a unique role as the sole authorities in the jungle areas. However, when British troops arrived to resume authority months after the Japanese capitulation, the guerrillas were shunted aside and ordered to surrender their weapons.

The majority of the guerrillas were Chinese immigrants who had come to work the tin mines and rubber plantations before the war. During the war, when the mines and plantations were largely shut down, many of the immigrants had built themselves homesteads on the fringes of the jungle where they had remained as squatters.

In 1948, when the Kremlin ordered its minions in the colonial areas to begin their "liberation wars," they again took to the woods to continue the struggle against the British.

The thick jungle provided the necessary safe bases for the guerrillas. The British and Americans during the war against Japan had provided them with weapons which they had hidden away when the British returned. Raids on police stations and barracks could produce the ammunition needed. But in one respect, food, they were vulnerable. Mao Tse-tung had taught that guerrillas based in rural areas could rely on the peasantry for food. The trouble was the jungle was not really a rural area in the sense of being a food producing area of cultivated fields. Furthermore, the "peasants" were in fact aboriginals whose tiny plots had never produced more than enough to maintain their own families.

To make up for this deficiency the guerrillas had to depend on their supporters in the towns and villages to collect food and transport it into the jungle. This civilian element organized into a Communist-led association known as the Min Yuen relied at first on voluntary contributions for their food, but as the campaign progressed this became more and more difficult. Gradually terror became the chief method of making collections. Villagers who did not produce their quota of food were brutally beaten up, their homes burned, their sons abducted for the guerrilla units.

Because of the difficulty of procuring large quantities of food regularly, the guerrillas were forced to break up the large units, which they had overambitiously formed, into small bands or platoons widely scattered along the jungle edge. This dispersal in turn prevented them from concentrating forces large enough to carry out substantial raids, ambushes or other offensive strikes essential to wearing down the enemy prior to entering the second phase of guerrilla war as taught by Mao.

As a result, most of the activities of the Malay guerrillas were purely terrorist. Nevertheless, these activities were enough to disrupt the economic life of Malaya for years. Plantation and mine managers were murdered and their workers terrorized into leaving their jobs. Malay politicians and police who collaborated with the British were likewise threatened with assassination, arson and abduction.

The British military had learned the art of jungle fighting during the war against the Japanese. They understood that the only way to combat jungle guerrillas was to adopt their tactics and, by constantly raiding their camps in small mobile units, to disband them. But when the big camps were broken up and the guerrillas dispersed into small bands of eight or ten men each, these tactics too were futile. Despite their helicopters and other airborne techniques, the British were unable to put enough troops into the jungle to catch the tiny bands.

After several years of this hopeless struggle the British finally resorted to a strategy of attacking the guerrillas at their most vital point—the food supplies which had to come from the villages and towns beyond the jungle. The aim was to isolate them both psychologically and physically from the rest of the population.

Ever since the British had returned to Malaya they had attempted to pursue a policy of flexibility and tolerance where social reforms could be effective and of firmness only when firmness was unavoidable. For instance they recognized the right of labor to organize even though they knew the trade unions were under Communist control and they took legal action against the unions only when the Party resorted to extreme measures. Furthermore, they were attentive to real grievances of the workers, Malay, Indian and Chinese, and in the end somewhat reluctantly speeded up the process of granting national independence, thereby winning over the Malayan natives.

But the Chinese squatters, always distrustful of government in any form, were less amenable and continued to remain loyal to their cousins in the jungle. Only physical isolation could cut the supply line from the villages or outlying squatter compounds to the jungle camps. Thus began the process of pre-dawn raids rounding up the inhabitants of recalcitrant settlements and individual homesteads and herding them into armed camps such as Kampong Jalong where they were guarded day and night by British troops and Malay police.

Needless to say, these village-camps were not at first popular and did little to persuade their inhabitants that the guards were their friends and the guerrillas in the surrounding jungle their enemies. Furthermore, it was almost physically impossible despite the fences and gates to seal off the villagers hermetically. The long-range aim of the antiguerrilla operation was after all to restore order and normal economic life. For this the mines and plantations had to be operated and the workers had to be permitted to go out of the village to work them. It was a relatively simple matter for the hostile villagers to hide sacks of potatoes under their clothes as they went to work and conceal them in a drying shed or bury them by the jungle's edge where the guerrillas could later send patrols to fetch them.

To prevent this, central cooking facilities were set up in the camps where the villagers were fed in mess halls in which the food was concentrated and guarded. Workers going out to the plantations were not even allowed to take food for their noonday meals. Periodic raids on their huts discouraged them from hoarding sufficient food to carry into the fields. Even medicines were rationed to the daily needs of each family.

But such measures were costly in manpower and provided no permanent solution. Furthermore, the most stringent measures could not prevent the villagers from supplying the bandits with another commodity essential to their survival—intelligence. Every movement of troops, every patrol, every ambush was carefully observed by the village sympathizers and quickly communicated to the guerrillas.

The British soon realized that to isolate the guerrillas effectively, more sophisticated measures than mere physical isolation were necessary. Somehow by a combination of education and coercion the villagers must be persuaded that support of the guerrillas was futile and co-operation with the authorities, in the long run, more profitable.

The coercive measures were simple enough. Villages notorious for their aid to the bandits were blacklisted and punished with rigid curfew laws and strict food rationing. In contrast, villages which co-operated were put on the "white list," given greater freedom of movement and more food and supplies.

Education was a more delicate task. The problem was that the Chinese immigrants who formed the bulk of the bandit support were by tradition hostile to constituted authority. The only officials they knew were tax collectors or policemen. What loyalties they had were to the home and the family—many of whose members were absent in the jungle. If they joined any organization at all it was to protect their family interests, not to co-operate with the authorities. The idea of community self-government or protection was completely alien to them.

This was the situation when Major John and his infantry battalion were ordered from Australia to occupation duty in Malaya. When he received his orders, John's first step was to telegraph the British authorities in Malaya for instructors to explain the local situation to him and to his officers and men. On the troop ship transporting them north, his soldiers were subjected to an intensive briefing in the problems they were to encounter. Not only were they instructed on guerrilla and counterinsurgent tactics but also they were told about the background and customs, the traditions and taboos of the people with whom they were to deal —Malay, Chinese and Indians.

When John arrived in Kampong Jalong it was notoriously pro-Communist and high on the "black list." Running it was a four-man team consisting of the local Malayan civil affairs officer, the local police chief, a political information officer and himself. This team system, set up by General Templer who had been sent out from England when the bandit problem was at its worst, was in John's opinion one of the most valuable contributions to the successful implementation of the pacification program.

One of John's first aims was to show the villagers that his

troops were not hostile occupiers but well-disposed protectors. Wisely he started his popularity campaign with the children. Building playgrounds and recreation facilities, his soldiers organized sports competitions, boxing matches and other games. Once the children were won over he turned to their parents. Careful to channel all his suggestions and orders through the native civil affairs officer, he avoided any semblance of being a colonial administrator. Never once in his stay did he directly issue an order affecting internal security arrangements. This he did through the local police chief.

But winning over the villagers was slow work. Everyone was hostile and unco-operative when he first arrived. Even the highly intelligent local schoolteacher, San Bin, an educated man, who should have understood what the community's interests were, seemed indifferent to John's efforts at friendliness.

But on the military side John's activities were less dependent on local good will. He built a good road around the perimeter of the plantation area and established outposts so that motorized patrols could reach any point on the perimeter within a few minutes. Each day he launched patrols into the jungle, always at different places, always with the greatest secrecy so that the villagers and hence the bandits could not find out in advance where his units might be prowling. Each day patrols carefully inspected the sheds and other hide-outs in the plantation where food for the guerrillas might be cached.

One of these search parties eventually provided the break which finally solved the "education" problem in the person of the schoolteacher San Bin. In one of the drying sheds where the raw rubber was stored, one of his soldiers discovered three containers of potatoes obviously hidden for the guerrillas. That very night Major John organized an ambush.

Luckily there was a full moon. An officer and four men were posted around the shed so that they could watch a small footbridge leading to it across a creek beyond which lay the jungle.

Well-trained in ambush techniques the soldiers waited silently in the shadows until six shapes emerged from the heavy undergrowth at the far end of the narrow bridge. Five of them approached the bridge walking single file. The sixth remained lurking on the far bank. The five were almost across when they made a rush toward the shed. At that instant the Australian officer gave the order to fire. Four of the bandits were killed instantly. The fifth somehow managed to get around the shed and disappear but not before he had been hit.

When the four dead bandits were brought into the village they were quickly identified by their relatives. Next morning Major John sent out a search party for the fifth man and it found him not far in the jungle, alive but seriously wounded in the neck. A woman was trying to dress his wound. Carefully hiding the wounded prisoner and the woman in a closed truck, the patrol brought them to Major John. John was not too surprised to discover they were none other than the schoolteacher, San Bin, and his wife. Wisely overcoming the temptation to announce publicly that San Bin had been caught red-handed with the bandits, he shipped him off secretly to a rehabilitation school run by the British military.

For three months San Bin was cared for until his wound healed. All the time he was subjected to intensive schooling. By the time he was well San Bin was a convinced anti-Communist. Back in the village, his absence unexplained, San Bin was one of the first to reverse the flow of information from the guerrillas to the troops. Gradually, too, he managed to persuade his fellow villagers of the futility of further supporting the bandits.

Before Major John's assignment to Kampong Jalong was over, the village had been taken off the black list of bandit-supporting communities and put on the white list. Its curfew was raised, its food rationing discontinued. So far as Major John knows it is still on the white list.

In a sense, the British counterinsurgent strategy in Malaya was a contradiction of Magsaysay's counterguerrilla operation in the Philippines. Instead of removing grievances, it created a new one—that of forcing reluctant peasants to abandon their homes and plots and be herded into armed detention camps.

This disadvantage was overcome in part by a special mitigating circumstance, in part by a vigorous campaign of civic action and indoctrination. The Chinese squatters, whom the strategy chiefly affected, had not been attached to their lands for generations. Many, indeed, had taken them over during the war years when food supplies under the Japanese occupation had run low in the towns and work on the plantations and in the mines had been drastically curtailed. Their attachment to the soil was therefore considerably less than one might expect in other rural communities, although it required the use of considerable guile backed by force to round them up.

Secondly, as Sir Gerald Templer, the High Commissioner, repeatedly stressed in his semi-annual reports, the strategy was by no means confined to forced resettlement but a major effort was made to winning over "the hearts and minds of the Malayan people."

His first step was to insist that the British government definitely commit itself to granting Malayan independence—the one cause the Communists might effectively exploit to unite the population against his regime. Thereafter the Communist influence was largely confined to the Chinese community—particularly the more recently arrived Chinese squatters. Furthermore, as soon as the squatters were delivered to their new villages, the four-man teams like Major John's went to work to wean their sympathies from their cousins and brothers in the jungle.

Templer's first appeal was to their material needs. The new villages were not only close to the places of work on the plantations nearby but they were better laid out, better constructed and better supplied with community facilities than their miserable homesteads on the jungle's edge. While the community houses, playgrounds and schools were being built to win over their children, the adults were constantly urged to assume responsibility not just over their individual households but over the whole village. Local guard units were organized and armed—though at first with considerable hesitation. Moreover, while British troops had been used to round up the squatters, native Malayan civil affairs officers spearheaded, at least ostensibly, the self-improvement civic action programs and thus gained credit for whatever progress was achieved.

Nor did Templer's teams ignore propaganda techniques. While they were well equipped with loudspeakers, printing press and photo labs, they soon learned that, unless they had successes to exploit, the gadgets were of little use. When Major John was able to photograph an emaciated guerrilla captured in the jungle and a few weeks later juxtapose it with a picture of the same guerrilla fattened and happy after a stay in a rehabilitation center, the two photos were distributed in the jungle as widely as possible. But when London sent learned scripts or pamphlets on the relative merits of democracy and Communism, they rapidly found their way into the Major's scrap basket.

Nevertheless, the re-education of the Chinese squatters was a slow process. Initially most of the new villagers flatly refused to have anything to do with the community's administration or even to participate in its self-defense. But little by little their suspicions were reduced and slowly they began to co-operate in community projects. In the end practically all the villages were guarded by the villagers themselves so that the police and the troops could be free to pursue guerrillas through the jungle.

Eventually, the British strategy not only defeated Moscow's bid for power in Malaya but produced a pattern of community life more stable, more integrated and better able to defend itself than any that had existed when the emergency began.

Because of these achievements, the British isolation operation in Malaya has become a model of counterinsurgent strategy, particularly for those responsible for dealing with the Communist guerrillas in South Vietnam. It might therefore be useful to analyze the balance sheet of Malaya a little more closely.

The first feature that strikes one is the very small number of guerrillas or bandits involved. It has been estimated that at the height of its activity the Communist guerrilla force comprised only about 5000 armed men and perhaps 500 women. (It is estimated that in Vietnam today there are nearly 20,000 armed guerrillas.) Against them the British were able to deploy 40,000 regular troops, 25,000 of which were British, and about 100,000 regular and auxiliary police both native and British including Scotland Yard. Thus there was a ratio of guerrillas to counterinsurgents of about one to twenty-five.

The political and economic costs to the British were even higher. At the beginning of the trouble, London had had no intention of giving up its rich and prosperous colonies in Malaya, which produced much of the world's tin and rubber. But before the emergency was ended, it had to grant them complete independence. As a result the British economy had to forego most of the rich revenues it formerly derived from Malaya's tin mines and rubber plantations.

Thirdly, despite these sacrifices it took the British more than ten years to break the insurgents' hold. In fact, in 1958, ten years after Moscow had ordered its liberation war, guerrilla bands were still roaming the Malayan jungle.

To be sure, the British had to contend with guerrillas in a terrain ideally suited to irregular warfare, but the Malay Communists too fought under severe handicaps. The most important perhaps was the absence of a foreign base of support. British intelligence sources found little evidence that the guerrillas received any substantial supplies from China or the Soviet Union even in the form of money. The guerrillas had no direct land communication with other Communist-controlled areas and the seaways were usually successfully interdicted by the British navy and air force.

But as we have noted perhaps their greatest handicap was that the rural areas of Malaya, which according to classical Communist doctrine should have provided them with their food supplies, were not really food-producing at all. And the aborigines who inhabited the jungle were not peasants but the most primitive, uneducated savages with few political concepts which Communist propaganda could exploit.

A further handicap was the antagonism between the three major races—Malayans, Indians and Chinese—which had existed long before the war broke out and which the British were able to exploit to isolate the predominantly Chinese Communist movement. With the exception of the universal aspiration for independence shared by all Malayans, most of the population had few grievances with the colonial administration after the initial chaos which followed the Japanese surrender. When the Kremlin ordered the Party to start its armed insurrection, the tin mines had been restored to operation and the rubber plantations were enjoying a boom so that the country was in a prosperous state.

The British too were the fortuitous beneficiaries of blunders by the Communists themselves. In one sense the greatest blunder was the Kremlin's calling its followers in Malaya to arms in a struggle which had so little hope of success. Though a superficial application of classical Communist guerrilla doctrines could conceivably have demonstrated that a "liberated Malaya" under Communist control was theoretically possible, a closer analysis would have shown the leaders in Moscow that the odds for success were exceedingly slim. Doubtless, in its call to arms which was sent out to all Southeast Asian parties, the Kremlin was far more interested in weakening the over-all military strength of the

Western Allies than in liberating its dark-skinned comrades. Though the effort in Malaya cost the Party 6000 dead and nearly 3000 surrendered or captured, it cost Moscow nothing except a local loss of prestige. On the other hand it kept 140,000 British troops and police tied down that might have been available in more critical areas in Europe or elsewhere just when the Soviet Union was deeply concerned with its own military weakness during the period of recovery immediately following World War II.

The Communist organization in Malaya was also severely handicapped by dissensions within its own ranks. Shortly before it took to the jungle its wartime leader, Lai Teck, was found to have collaborated with the Japanese and to have absconded with Party funds. He was expelled just as the call to arms reached the Party from Moscow.

Furthermore, though the Party itself was comparatively rich because of its domination of the trade unions, whose dues were a highly lucrative source of funds, the rank and file suspected that its leaders were living too well compared to the Party workers who were paid far less than they might have earned within the flourishing private economy. This naturally led to distrust and discontent among the lower ranks.

Finally the blunders of the Communist command in the interpretation of Mao Tse-tung's rules, which we have already mentioned, played directly into British hands. The inadequate supply system, the inability of the guerrillas to progress from terrorism to larger-scale guerrilla operations and their dependence on only the Chinese minority in Malaya, ably exploited by the British, were major factors in their final defeat.

While all of these factors militating against the guerrillas were made full use of by the British in the campaign of isolation initiated by General Briggs and vigorously implemented by Sir Gerald Templer, they were neither created nor instigated by the

British but were inherent in the situation which they confronted.

They must therefore be discounted in applying the British strategy to other counterinsurgent operations in situations where they do not necessarily exist. For example, it would be a mistake to assume that the strategy of isolation in guarded villages will necessarily work in Vietnam without basic modifications just because it worked in Malaya. All that can be assumed is that the strategy of isolation may in given circumstances be successful.

Thus the basic lesson of the Malay counterinsurgent campaign is that given a vigorous government, a rebellious guerrilla force can be defeated by attrition if it is cut off from its base of supplies—in the case of Malaya, from the villages and villagers beyond the jungle's fringe. But this isolation cannot be achieved by force alone. Nor can it be confined to physical isolation. Without winning the voluntary collaboration of key elements in the population military measures alone seldom stop guerrillas.

VIII Terror

The little ship had hardly left the harbor at Rhodes when a violent storm struck it. For several days it floundered in the wind-ripped Mediterranean. Below deck its only passenger lay miserably seasick in his bunk. It was hardly the way he had imagined setting forth on his great crusade, a venture for which he had been planning and preparing himself for years.

Up on the bridge the captain of the vessel wondered who the mysterious passenger was for whom he had been paid so handsome a price to land him on the island of Cyprus. Even before they had left harbor he had found him to be a grim, humorless, taciturn little man who obviously considered himself very important.

Though he was not aware of it, the captain's opinion of Georg Grivas was shared by everyone who had known him since he had first attended the military academy in Athens back in 1916. Subsequently in the Turkish-Greek War Grivas' fellow officers had found him unsociable and withdrawn. He never smoked, drank or took part in their social life and as one of them said later, "No one could call him a friend."

Born in Nicosia on the island of Cyprus in 1898, the son of a grocer, he had always seemed ashamed of his simple origins. At least that was how his fellow officers explained his bitter, resentful attitude. Yet his colleagues respected him in a curious way. He was tireless and demanding, a martinet who required no less of himself than he did of the soldiers under him. He was ruthless too. Later, during the German invasion in 1941, it was said that in the headlong retreat he had shot all stragglers in his unit with his own pistol. In preparation for his present undertaking, he had trained himself to subsist on a diet of fruit which he munched every hour. Twice a week he allowed himself a thin slice of cold meat.

During the German occupation he had organized a small underground group which he called Organization "X." Politically, "X" was an extreme Rightist, pro-Monarchist movement which attracted few followers and never amounted to very much though it directed its terrorist activities against both the German occupation and the Communist underground. When the Germans eventually retired, Grivas attached his little band to the British liberation forces and was several times almost annihilated by Communist guerrillas during the Communist uprising in 1944. Each time the British came to his rescue. Characteristically, he never subsequently showed any gratitude to the British for repeatedly saving his life.

When the Communist attempt to take over was suppressed in Athens and a caretaker government installed awaiting the plebiscite to determine whether the King was to be restored, the politicians who came to power in 1945 retired Grivas from the army because of his extreme Rightist views. Thus his professional career came to an end without honors or emoluments except for a tiny pension.

More embittered than ever, he entered politics himself and ran for Parliament but without success. His program was the restoration of the monarchy, and when this was achieved, without much contribution from him and without recognition for his services, he retired to a small apartment in the suburb of Thyssion in Athens. There he lived with his wife whom he had married after a courtship of eleven years.

Resigned to his fate, he took off his military boots for what he thought was the last time and told his wife to throw them away. But for some reason, she failed to do so.

Then for five long years he devoted himself to a careful study of the Communist movement, its organization and strategy, particularly its subversive activities, its guerrilla methods and its terrorist tactics. His interest in the subject was by no means academic. Despite his instructions to his wife about the boots, he seemed convinced, like most fanatics, that one day he would be called upon to render some signal service to his fatherland which would finally earn him the recognition he so hankered for.

He was not sure exactly what the mission might be but he toyed for a time with the idea of leading an Irredentist movement against southern Albania, or, as the Greeks called it, Northern Epirus, then in Communist hands. But he came into contact with the head of the Cypriot Orthodox Church and from that moment his mission was fixed—the liberation of his native Cyprus from British rule and its union with Greece.

The island, forty miles off the Turkish coast, was ethnically eighty per cent Greek with a Turkish minority of eighteen per cent stemming from the days when Turkey had ruled it from the sixteenth century. In 1821 the British had taken it over and had governed it ever since. After World War II and the subsequent withdrawal of the British from Egypt and Palestine it had become an important military and naval base for the Empire in the Middle East.

For decades the Greek majority in Cyprus had dreamed

vaguely of an eventual union with Greece. Oddly enough the Cypriot Orthodox Church had been the spearhead of the movement, and when the young bishop of Kitium became archbishop, with the title of Makarios III, he resolved that at last the time had come to realize the long-sought dream of Enosis—union with Greece—if necessary by force. "It is only through the exercise of violence that the British can be made to understand," he said. But Makarios III was shrewd enough to realize that the 400,000 Greek Cypriots crowded on a small island were no match for the British Empire in any sort of fair fight. What form then was the violence to take? It was at this point that Makarios came into contact with Grivas, who had the answer and a detailed plan of action.

The plan called for unlimited terror against the British forces on Cyprus in three stages: first the blowing up of police stations, barracks and radio installations. The second stage was to be directed against Cypriot Greeks who failed to acknowledge the leadership of the terrorist-guerrillas. "Traitors" to the cause of Greek union and collaborators of the British were to be assassinated. In the final stage terror was to be directed against the British forces themselves, their officers, soldiers and even families.

From his study of Communism, Grivas knew that before even the first stage could be put into operation careful preparations had to be made—not simply the caching of arms but more important the recruiting and training of his guerrilla bands. Unfortunately for him and his collaborator Archbishop Makarios, the civilian population of Cyprus was enjoying an almost unprecedented economic prosperity under British rule. Few mature Cypriots were in a mood to sacrifice their material comforts for an effort to oust the British government. Partly for this reason Grivas had discarded the idea of a traditional guerrilla revolt which would necessitate a mass uprising, for at best he could count on only a small minority to play an active role.

Also from his study of Communist doctrine, Grivas knew that

the most vulnerable element, the most easily indoctrinated following would be the young people between the ages of seventeen and twenty-five. But to inculcate even the youth with sufficient fanaticism to carry out his cold-blooded terror was a major problem.

Fortunately, his allies and in a sense his employers, the Orthodox priests, provided the answer. For they were in a position to organize and imbue the youth with the devotion and discipline which Grivas' plans called for.

Two years before his stormy passage from Rhodes, Grivas had surreptitiously visited Makarios in Cyprus and prescribed the form of youth organization and the type of indoctrination. He urged that the young men be required to take a secret oath to the cause of Enosis, vowing complete dedication to it and declaring their readiness to sacrifice their lives and never to reveal the secrets of the conspiracy even under torture.

Makarios and his priests zealously put these suggestions into operation. The cause of Enosis was preached openly in sermons. Secretly, promising young men were recruited and given the oath—often by the priests themselves.

Even after Grivas' landing in 1954 much still remained to be done. For six months he worked night and day, organizing and training bands of five to ten men each in the art of demolition, collecting and caching weapons and explosives, preparing hideouts and establishing an intricate system of couriers, cut-outs and codes to be used when the day came

By January 1955, internal preparations were ready but still one thing was lacking: an external base and source of supplies. Only Greece could provide this but its Prime Minister, Field Marshal Papagos, was reluctant to support the movement and incur the enmity of Greece's traditional friends, the British. Only after constant pressure from Makarios was Papagos reluctantly won over.

In the end Papagos promised the use of Radio Athens as a

source of propaganda and the facilities of Greek territory for the acquisition and forwarding of munitions. On March 29, 1954, Makarios gave Grivas the order to start.

At the appointed hour Grivas was in hiding in a suburb of Nicosia, the capital of Cyprus, waiting anxiously for the first blow —the cutting of Nicosia's main power lines. When the moment came, the light in his hide-out flickered but then glowed again as steady as ever. Grivas was furious at this inauspicious beginning. Nor was he mollified when he got the explanation: the young man who had been assigned to cut the mains had electrocuted himself in the attempt.

But elsewhere on the island the first stage of sabotage was more successful. A number of police stations were blown up and bombs exploded in public places. In the schools riots took place; teachers who refused to condone the movement were beaten up and leaflets signed "Dighenis" (the name of a Greek mythological hero Grivas had assumed) were distributed in the towns by the students.

Within weeks the movement entered its second stage. Cypriots who refused to support the movement were murdered in cold blood, their shops wrecked, their homes destroyed. By October the island was in a state of panic. The British government sent one of its most able World War II generals, Field Marshal Sir John Harding, to the island as governor and with him 300 extra British police to re-enforce the troops.

But Grivas' well-indoctrinated and trained bands of fanatics continued to sabotage and murder. At the end of October the campaign entered its third stage when a British soldier was assassinated. In December 1955, Sir John declared a state of emergency, which was to last until March of 1959.

For four long years the grim little sadist waged the most ruthless and vicious of terrorist wars. His fortunes varied. After several months of spectacular successes he had been able to enlist the open support of many Cypriots, especially among the young people, and to coerce the remainder to heed his orders. Those who were foolish enough to refuse were reported to Grivas in his hideout and their names entered on the liquidation list. Few thus listed survived.

Field Marshal Harding was no less active. But his efforts were confined chiefly to the police and the military for at that stage London, obsessed with anachronistic views of the importance of Cyprus as a military base, had no intention of granting it independence in any form. Thus Harding was in no position to make concessions which might have undercut Grivas' support among the youth for whom Independence had a powerful appeal. By 1956 Makarios' role in the terrorist campaign had become so notorious that the British were forced to arrest him and exile him to the Seychelles islands. The expulsion caused considerable resentment among the Cypriots and produced a new wave of sympathy for the terrorist Grivas. Already the poorer elements of the population had succumbed to his threats and now the richer Cypriots turned against the British.

Frustrated by the ease with which Grivas' assassins could commit murder in the heart of Nicosia in broad daylight without a single witness willing to testify, Harding ordered mass searches of whole areas. Rich Cypriots who had been at least not unfriendly to the British were indignant when they were roughly ordered from their cars to be searched by British troops. Sometimes hundreds of suspects were rounded up in mass arrests and held for days while a handful of interpreters attempted to interrogate them. These and other indignities soon turned the last of the Cypriots against the British.

In April of 1956 for the first time a British civilian was assassinated. A Turkish policeman was shot and a bomb was discovered under Field Marshal Harding's bed, placed there by an apparently loyal Cypriot servant who had been recruited by Grivas' agents.

In May and June of 1956, Harding mounted a major operation in the mountains where Grivas was known to be hiding. Grivas himself was encircled and several times almost captured, but each time using his carefully planned chain of hide-outs he was able to escape detection while he hid in a concealed cave, a monastery or under the false floor of a peasant house.

Nevertheless, Harding's offensive bagged a number of terrorist leaders and their followers, and Grivas' communications system, always slow, was seriously disrupted. His terror tactics too began to repel decent Cypriots. Some began to turn informer which resulted in further serious casualties among the terrorist bands. Grivas' hold over the population seemed to be slipping.

Just as he was considering calling for a truce while he reorganized his forces and trained new recruits to replace his casualties he got the respite he needed. The Suez crisis came to a head and Harding was forced to suspend his operations and send many of his troops and equipment to the canal zone. By the fall of 1956, Grivas' reorganization was completed and his murders of disloyal Cypriots had been resumed. Between July and December of that year no fewer than sixty-six Cypriot "traitors" were killed.

But at the beginning of 1957, the tide again turned against the guerrillas. In January two of Grivas' closest collaborators were killed and a number of his best terrorists captured. Again Grivas found it necessary to rest and reorganize his killers. He asked for a truce, which was accepted. But by July he had recuperated again and resumed his savagery. In November of that year, a Turkish policeman was blown up on the way to his wedding with his fiancée. The indignant Turkish community began to show signs of unrest.

At this point Sir John Harding was recalled and replaced by a diplomat, Sir Hugh Foote. At the same time London showed signs that it might be willing to discuss Cypriot independence—provided the terror subsided. Thus the new governor was at last in a position to take a fresh political approach. Stressing his civilian character, Foote moved about freely among the population daring Grivas to attack him. At the same time he initiated a vigorous propaganda campaign against Grivas in which he depicted the terrorist as a madman who was driving Cyprus to suicide. The campaign had its effect and once more Grivas found his hold on the population slipping. Guided by his always unreliable political instinct Grivas lashed out against the liberal Cypriot Left, thereby alienating a major element of the population. Then he ordered the blowing up of a government agricultural installation on which many Cypriot farmers depended. Thus he lost more backing.

Meantime Foote secretly offered to meet Grivas face to face to try to negotiate a settlement. Timidly Grivas refused. But by then the Turkish minority, enraged by a bomb which destroyed the Turkish Information Office, started to riot. A number of British soldiers were assassinated. Then a Mrs. Cutliffe, the wife of a British soldier, was shot down while shopping in Nicosia. In retaliation British troops for a moment lost their composure and fired on helpless civilians.

Thoroughly alarmed, the British government in London publicly offered Cyprus its independence under joint Turkish-Greek rule while retaining the right to maintain a British military base on the island. The Turkish government at once accepted but the Greeks hesitated. This was not Enosis—indeed it was an offer much resembling one London had offered earlier but which had been scornfully rejected by Makarios.

Meanwhile on the island the military commander under Foote put a curfew on the movements of all young men. Severe rules were established for the movement of workers from their homes to their places of work. The population saw the island's economic life grinding to a halt. Surfeited by terror and hardships they again began to turn away from Grivas and Makarios. At last the

e farmer, for failure to provide food for the Huks. In the
War, native shopkeepers were frequently ordered to
nds in a rebel hide-out or face death.

 guerrillas resort to terror to enforce discipline within
 camp. Tito's official biographer, Vladimir Dedijer, in
Tito Speaks describes how two Partisan soldiers were
ed to death for stealing food from a peasant woman. Ac-
o Dedijer, before they were shot one of the condemned
e a speech approving the sentence because he had sullied
name of the Partisan movement. In Malaya the Commu-
illas frequently kidnaped young men to swell their own
l forced them to fight by the simple expedient of threat-
hoot them or their families if they deserted.

unterpart of terror when used by the counterinsurgent is
Its purpose is of course to discourage further acts of
Reprisal can be as mild as collective fines imposed on a
ty where a terrorist act has been committed. It can in-
 shooting of hundreds of innocent enemy civilians in
n for every counterinsurgent killed. As we have seen,
ans successfully persuaded Mikhailovitch's force to de-
acts of sabotage against the occupation because of fear
l against either their families at home in Belgrade or
e villagers who supported the Chetniks in the provinces.
ase of the Partisans, however, reprisal was singularly
e for reasons we have examined. In their case it merely
d recruitment and increased the determination of the
l Partisan to destroy the Nazis. Similarly, German re-
iled completely to deter the Soviet Partisans in Russia in
ar II.

vas' movement demonstrated, terror and its counterpart,
are dangerous double-edged weapons. Though they may
bedience through fear they seldom enlist sympathetic
Whenever Grivas' acts of sabotage overstepped the limits

Archbishop found himself compelled to accept a solution which
fell far short of his goal. Reluctantly he abandoned Enosis and
accepted the British offer of joint Greek-Turkish rule.

Grivas, still in hiding, was stunned by what he considered
Makarios' treachery. But he realized that without the help of the
Cypriot Church he could not survive. Offered a safe conduct by
the British, he put on the best face he could, emerged from his
hiding place under the nose of the British police in Nicosia and
boarded a plane for Athens. There for a brief moment he was
welcomed as a hero. He was even invited to luncheon by King
Paul. For some days he enjoyed the homage of the populace but
little by little the adulation waned as the Greek public recalled the
hideous suffering his savagery had caused their compatriots in
Cyprus. Gradually he slid into obscurity where he still survives,
no longer the hero he had dreamed of becoming.

Grivas' campaign in Cyprus is instructive for a number of
reasons. In several respects Grivas thoroughly learned his lessons
in the study of Communist rebellions. Before he finally decided to
devote himself to Enosis, he had, as we have noted, considered
other possible irredenta—specifically Northern Epirus or Southern Albania. But he seems to have concluded correctly that a
liberation movement in an area already under Communist control, with its highly efficient and ruthless police system, stood
little chance of success. On the other hand a campaign to reduce
England's "will to rule" in Cyprus had real promise.

England had already demonstrated in India and Africa that
her imperial ambitions were waning. The importance of Cyprus
as a military base in the age of atom bombs was likewise dimin-
ishing. And the need for such a base in the Near East, where the
Empire's vital interests had been shrinking, was likewise
dwindling.

One might well ask why Grivas limited himself to terror, the
most restricted form of guerrilla warfare, instead of aiming at an

eventual mass uprising. A study of previous movements seems to have shown him that on a small, heavily populated island, well patrolled by an efficient though humane police and far from his source of supply across the sea in Greece, large guerrilla bands could hardly hope to find the bases for training, rest and recruiting which a growing guerrilla operation requires. Furthermore, even he seemed to doubt whether the cause of Enosis would have sufficient appeal to the mass of Cypriots to persuade them to forego their current prosperity in pursuit of unification with Greece.

Hence he had to limit himself to a few small, well-trained bands of young men who when pursued could take refuge in the ingeniously disguised hide-outs he had prepared in advance and supplied with food and ammunition. These were Grivas' substitutes for the bases a more substantial guerrilla force would have required.

Whether his reliance on terror alone was as wisely placed is another matter. History provides few cases where terror by itself has been successful in achieving a major political aim.

Terror has been defined as the attempt to govern or to oppose government by intimidation, or as the threat or the use of violence for political ends. The violence may range from burning crosses on political opponents' front lawns to sabotage, the burning of villages, kidnaping, assassination and mutilation.

Ordinarily, guerrillas resort to violence of this nature only when other forms of irregular warfare are denied them by lack of followers or lack of suitable weapons. Thus it is, as Brian Crozier has said, a weapon of the weak. If and when the guerrilla force grows in numbers and strength, terror assumes a less important role. In the case of Grivas, his movement never graduated from terror.

Terror can be used against the enemy to destroy his will to resist as Grivas tried to use it against British soldiers and police and finally against British civilians. But against a resolute enemy, terror of this nature seldom succeeds and, as Grivas discovered,

by its very horror it often increases th conjunction with other circumstance against the British in Palestine in 1 Canal zone in 1954 when the cost of the value of the objective in dispute. far from a complete failure for thoug it did force the British to grant inde

Against a government more ruthle terror is less successful. Where one sassination loses much of its value. N in terror of assassins and when his fr 1934 he let loose one of the greatest history. Whether his successors or th would react with equal violence, wei assassinated, is questionable. But it is used effectively to divert them from to modify their current policies.

In non-Soviet areas terror is more native population or elements of it guerrillas and either remain passive o On the island of Cyprus the majority British or even Turkish but Greek C native Malayans were murdered tha many more Kikuyu tribesmen wer than whites.

In such cases the purpose of terror but more important to discourage ot and to encourage contributions to the 1955, Archbishop Makarios demar headmen in Cyprus resign. During th in five complied with his demand. murdered three of the recalcitrants. of every five headmen had resigned.

In an earlier chapter we noted the

Philippi
Algeria
deposit
Final
their ow
his bool
condem
cording
men ma
the goo
nist gue
ranks a
ening to
The c
reprisal.
rebellion
commu
volve th
retributi
the Ger
sist fron
of repri
against
In the
ineffecti
stimula
individu
prisals f
World
As G
reprisal,
enforce
support.

of patience of the civilian population which suffered indirectly therefrom, and especially whenever his murders exceeded in their brutality the tolerance of his fellow Cypriots, his support dwindled even though his orders continued to be obeyed.

Similarly in Palestine, both the Stern gang and the Irgun terrorists periodically were condemned by the more moderate elements of the Jewish population whenever their outrages became too savage even for their fellow Jews. During the Mau Mau terror in Kenya the most appalling mutilations were regularly performed on victims before they were finally put to death. But when in March of 1953 hundreds of Kikuyus were burned alive, pregnant women disemboweled and children chopped to pieces, even former native supporters of the movement were so revolted that according to one expert the Mau Mau movement thenceforth began to lose ground which it never recovered.

Inevitably, terror when countered by reprisal provokes more brutal terror which in turn brings down more ferocious reprisals. However, this escalation also has its limits.

As we have just noted, the Kikuyus in Kenya who were unimpressed by murder à la Grivas were terrorized only when murder was embellished by indescribable atrocities. Yet as just noted even these savage tribesmen apparently had standards below which terrorism became intolerable.

Without embarking upon a discussion of the moral or ethical justification of terror, it is relevant to examine the varying levels of tolerance of communities in the modern world.

During World War II, Prussian-trained Wehrmacht officers recoiled from the savage reprisals Hitler ordered and his SS troops executed against Russian Partisans, civilians and prisoners of war. Soviet officers, on the other hand, indoctrinated in a school not far removed from that of the Nazis, showed far less compunction in dealing with anti-Soviet Partisans and disaffected civilians in the Ukraine.

A century ago, the British and French were not squeamish in putting down rebellions by the most harsh treatment. Even during the Algerian War, French troops resorted to such brutal tactics in their treatment of prisoners of war that the French population at home was appalled when the details were made public.

At the turn of the century when, as described in an earlier chapter, an American general was sent against a group of Philippine guerrillas who had massacred almost an entire company of United States infantry, with orders to kill "everything over ten years old" in the guerrilla-infested area, the American public and specifically the Congress were so shocked that the general was recalled and court-martialed.

During World War II, an American Democratic Party politician was visiting the Yugoslav front toward the end of the war. The Partisan commander, anxious to demonstrate the perfidy of the Croatian Ustachi terrorist bands, brought forward a group of native Croatian prisoners captured in civilian clothes while allegedly fighting on the side of the Germans. When in answer to the American politician's question he explained that they were sentenced to death as *franc-tireurs* under the Hague rule of war, the American protested, appalled: "But you can't do that! They're just like our Republicans."

Though it is often argued that terror requires counterterror, the question arises whether the average American or British officer, trained in the venerable tradition of military chivalry, is capable of the cold-blooded brutality which terror or counterterror requires of its practitioners. The Western military man may well be inclined to consider the terrorist as nothing but an ordinary criminal. But whether he is capable of challenging the terrorist to a duel with his own weapons is more questionable. It would seem from past experience that American and particularly congressional objections would be similarly difficult to overcome. When Grivas shot stragglers in World War II, he was admired by his compatriots. When in the same war, an American general slapped the face of a soldier who, he believed, was shirking his duty the general narrowly escaped court-martial.

A former Jewish terrorist who saw service both under the Russian Partisans and in Palestine has argued cogently that the only antidote for terror is unlimited counterterror or reprisal. To fight terror in any less brutal way, he maintains, is to fight an oil fire with water which simply spreads the conflagration. Nitroglycerine, he urges, is the only alternative. One wonders, however, whether this advice coming from a member of a race whose ethical standards and moral compassion are unquestioned is not the direct result of its shattering experiences under both Hitler and the anti-Semitic Stalin.

Unless and until a different moral climate is created among Americans as a result of a national calamity, such as a nuclear war, it would seem that we have little alternative but Magsaysay's or that of the British in Malaya to offer against modern guerrilla terror.

IX Guerrillas as Auxiliaries

On JUNE 29, 1941, the little village of X, about a hundred miles southwest of Moscow, seemed almost deserted. A lone Soviet soldier patrolled the wide muddy road between the peasant huts. But behind the covered windows of one of the huts it was anything but quiet. That afternoon I had driven down to the village from Moscow bringing with me a small child whose mother was a Russian peasant girl, a native of X, and whose father was an American. Just seven days before, Germany had launched her invasion of Russia. In Moscow many people were recalling the savage air raids on Warsaw during the German attack on Poland, and the child's parents had asked me to take her to her maternal grandfather's home in X.

Rumors of the initial German breakthrough had already stirred the village. The very fact that "they," the government, had stationed a patrol of security troops in it, and imposed a curfew which the soldier was enforcing, indicated that Stalin was uneasy about the loyalty of his subjects.

But the patrol and the curfew were contemptuously ignored by the villagers. As soon as it was dark, a stream of bearded men had crept through the garden behind my hut and slipped in the door to hear the latest news of the war. I told them what we had learned of the extent of the German advance.

The old peasants smiled through their beards and winked at each other: "At last!" one of them said, and they all repeated the phrase. I looked at my host perplexed and asked what they meant. Throughout its long history Russia had been defended by its peasants against all invaders, as Napoleon had learned. Had the Bolshevik regime so embittered them that they were now actually welcoming a foreign invasion?

The old grandfather turned on me impatiently: "Just let the Kremlin give us some guns and we'll know whom to shoot," he said and shook his fist toward the window outside which the Red soldier was patrolling. Just to be sure I had not misunderstood he went on: "When Hitler comes across the bridge at the foot of the village, we'll all be out there to greet him with bread and salt."

In the spring of 1944, Field Marshal Busch, commanding the German Army Group Center, was given an impression of the Russian peasantry diametrically opposite to the one I had received in the peasant hut three years earlier. At that time the Army Group's line ran in the shape of a giant question mark gulping eastward in the north around Vitebsk, Orsha and Bobruisk, swinging back westward and then southward toward Pulsk and Rovno. The Field Marshal's intelligence service reported that a Russian build-up for a new offensive was under way and he expected it to strike at any time. But would they strike in the north around Vitebsk or in the south where the line swung several hundred miles to the west?

A series of probing attacks on the southern sector seemed to confirm the Field Marshal's suspicion that the offensive could be expected there. So hurriedly he shifted his reserves on the one rail-line available which ran from Vitebsk through Minsk to his southern sector.

His communications had been severely harassed by Partisans for months before he decided to shift his reserves to the south. Nearly 5000 breaks had been blown in the tracks by guerrillas and about 1200 railroad locomotives had been destroyed. But now, mercifully, the Partisans were once more quiet and for several weeks the line was untouched, permitting him to make the shift in record time. It was almost as though the guerrillas were being co-operative for once.

A nasty thought crossed the Field Marshal's mind but he dismissed it as he sat back and waited for the artillery bombardment that always preceded a Russian attack. He had not long to wait but when it came the Red artillery struck in the north between Vitebsk and Bobruisk. Hastily the Field Marshal ordered his reserves back up from the south and the troop trains started their long pull back through Minsk.

Then the Partisans struck with a vengeance. In the space of a single day they staged no less than 10,000 raids on the German communications lines. All troop movements from the south were completely stopped, leaving the northern sector without reserves. When the Russian infantry began its advance, the thinly held lines broke and the Red troops swept forward in a mighty rush.

What had happened to the revolt of the Soviet peasantry? Why, instead of attacking their hated Communist government as they had vowed to as in the village of X, had they formed one of the greatest guerrilla forces the world had ever seen and crippled the German Army's communications and rear areas?

The answer to these questions provides a classic example of how to instigate a Partisan movement against yourself and how not to deal with it.

Soviet wartime and postwar literature on the Red Partisan movement in World War II suggests that the movement was a well-planned development, organized even before the German invasion. I would suggest it was nothing of the sort. It may be that the Soviet army had plans for leaving behind diversionists and espionage agents in the event that the German armies attacked and drove them out of their western territories, but that they had any thought of a mass Partisan movement such as subsequently developed seems unlikely. Even Stalin, though often kept in ignorance of disagreeable facts by his sycophantic entourage, must have learned in the first few days of the war the extent of the disaffection among the population. To have planned a mass Partisan movement in such an atmosphere would have been pipe-dreaming.

For the attitude of the peasants in the village of X at the outbreak of the war was not a local phenomenon. Indeed, in the Ukraine the disaffection was far more serious. As the Germans swept forward in their initial surge, they were greeted with the traditional peasant symbols of welcome: bread and salt. In the countryside and in the towns they were showered with flowers and hailed as liberators. Even within the Soviet army in those early summer days, desertions on a mass scale were common.

To use Mao's famous simile, the temperature of the water in the Soviet Union at the outbreak of war was ideal for spawning a Partisan movement *against* the Kremlin. The spirit of revolt was strong not only in the Ukraine and White Russia. In the newly conquered Baltic states, in Georgia, in predominantly Tartar Crimea, nationalist feelings against Moscow domination were strong.

In the countryside, the peasants were bitterly hostile to the collective farm system imposed by the Communist rulers. In the cities, workers disillusioned by long unfulfilled promises of a better life would have welcomed almost any change of regime. Even in Moscow many Russians among the educated classes, embittered by the senseless, brutal terror which had gripped the country since 1934, awaited the coming of the Nazis as liberators. In the army, which had itself been severely purged during Stalin's terror, high-ranking officers had good reason for loathing their Communist leaders.

It would not have been difficult for the German invaders to win the friendship and loyalty of these disaffected elements. The nationalists would have been satisfied with a degree of local autonomy. The peasants only wanted to be freed from the hated collective farms. In the factories the workers wanted only a minimal subsistence level and humane working conditions. Among the intellectuals even the limited freedoms Hitler permitted his own Germans would have been hailed as progress. To be treated like trustworthy patriots rather than potential traitors and to have been freed from the constant surveillance of political commissars would have been adequate for the Germans to win the generals' loyalty to a new order.

It is easily understandable that many political observers in Moscow in 1941—and not just Germans—predicted a rapid end of the Soviet regime after the German attack. Only the crassest stupidity of the Nazi leaders, their arrogant conceit and ridiculous theories of super races, could blind them to the fact that only one threat, one danger, could unite the Soviet peoples against them and arouse the traditional Russian patriotism in defense of the Moscow regime—the threat of a foreign despotism, the danger of becoming slaves to a foreign colonial power rather than to a domestic native tyrant.

Yet this is precisely the course Hitler chose. What is more, he made no effort to disguise his intentions. Nor could he plead, as he tried to do when the inevitable Russian fury struck, that he had been misinformed. His brilliant ambassador in Moscow, Count von der Schulenburg, the able German military attaché, General von Koestring, and many others knew precisely the mood of the Russian people and how it could be exploited. But only after the tide had turned against him did Hitler consent to a modification of his policy that would permit the exploitation of the anti-Stalinist mood of the Russians. By then, as we have noted, it was far too late.

In his original orders for the conquest of Russia, "Operation Barbarossa," and its economic exploitation, "Operation Oldenburg," Hitler outlined his plans for the colonization of the Ukraine which was to serve as Germany's breadbasket. To facilitate grain collection, the collective farms were to be continued. Excess manpower was to be rounded up and shipped to Germany to work in Hitler's munitions plants. Captured enemy personnel were to be put on sub-subsistence rations in prison camps. Jews were to be exterminated. Finally, when Russia was conquered, it was to become a German protectorate.

As for guerrillas, Hitler hardly gave them a passing mention: they were to be "ruthlessly liquidated by the troops in combat or while trying to escape."

When these schemes were broadcast by the German radio, those of us who heard them in Moscow almost suspected that Goebbels was working for the Kremlin.

In fairness to the German generals, these directives were neither approved by them nor in most instances carried out. The front line forces generally treated their captives and the civilian population as decently as circumstances permitted. But close behind the front lines came the Nazi political commissars and police and they put the directives into force with inhuman zeal.

The reaction of the population in White Russia and the Ukraine was inevitable and immediate. Apparently abandoned by the retreating armies of their own regime who as they departed drove off the herds of cattle and burned the villages and wheat fields, and then treated like savages by the conquerors who replaced them, the peasants had only one alternative. With a curse on both their houses the able-bodied men and women slated for slave labor in Germany fled to the swamps and forests. Their one aim was simply survival.

Stalin and his followers in the Party were quick to appreciate the implications of this double defection. If the wave of desertion was not to sweep over all of the Soviet Union it must be stopped at once. Furthermore, if Stalin was ever to regain control over the areas presently overrun by the Germans, the roaming bands of refugees in the forests must not be permitted to become the spearheads of anti-Communist and Ukrainian nationalist independence movements as they had become after World War I.

His fears were well founded. Many of the bands, particularly in the Ukraine, were indeed fiercely anti-Communist and determined to liberate their country from Moscow's yoke. As we noted in an earlier chapter, four years later when the Germans were finally driven out of Russia, these bands were still operating but now behind the Russian lines and against the Soviet forces. For several years after the defeat of Germany they were still roaming the swamps and forests making occasional sorties to assassinate a Soviet commissar or Party official or burn a public building or loot a State granary.

But except for these rabid Ukrainian and White Russian nationalists, Stalin and his followers early in the war somehow managed with the Communist genius for capturing popular movements to take over the leadership of the majority of the disaffected peasants and mobilize them into an effective anti-German Partisan movement. Within eleven days of the outbreak of war, Stalin broadcast to the people of the Soviet Union, appealing to their traditional patriotism and asking them to defend not the Homeland of World Revolution, as he had always referred to it in the past, but Mother Russia. It was a shrewd posture to strike, for Stalin, though a Georgian himself, knew that ever since the Tartar invasions the Russian people had always in the past rallied to the defense of their soil.

In his appeal he specifically gave orders "to foment guerrilla warfare everywhere, to blow up bridges and roads, to destroy telephone and telegraph communications, to set fire to forests, depots and trains.

"In occupied territories," he went on, "conditions must be made intolerable for the enemy and his collaborators. They must be pursued and annihilated wherever they are."

"Collaborators"? If any doubt remains that Stalin was aware of the mass desertions to the enemy in those early days before Hitler's arrogant directives drove the peasants into the woods, that word must dispel them.

Immediately following the speech, the Kremlin ordered disciplined Party members in areas destined to be abandoned by the retreating armies to remain behind and organize resistance groups. In areas already overrun, Party organizers were sent back through the lines or by parachute, armed with propaganda about German atrocities, real and fictional, and with orders to take command of any Partisan movements already in being.

Except for Communist literature, there is little available evidence on just how these Communist Party organizers gained control of the bands. The fact that many bands survived the war without submitting to Kremlin leadership suggests that the Party organizers were not universally welcomed. Stalin's own predilection for terror and the known activities of Party organizers in the French Maquis and among the anti-German guerrillas of northern Italy suggest that anti-Germany atrocity propaganda was not their only weapon. One cannot but suspect that, as in western Europe, assassination or execution of guerrilla leaders on trumped-up charges of collaboration was not unknown.

But whatever the means, German atrocities plus the zeal of Party organizers and the traditional patriotism of the Russian people succeeded in winning over thousands of guerrillas to harass the German invaders.

The demolition of the Orsha-Minsk-Brest railroad, which cost Field Marshal Busch so heavily, was only one of thousands of such operations. Lieutenant General Ponomarenko, in charge of Soviet guerrilla activities in the Kremlin, claims that in two years the guerrillas had killed over 300,000 Germans including 30 generals, derailed 3000 trains, destroyed 3263 rail and highway bridges, destroyed nearly a thousand ammunition and supply dumps and blown up nearly 10,000 vehicles. Another Soviet report says that during the course of the war in the Ukraine alone over 300,000 Germans were killed, 4000 locomotives destroyed and nearly 40,000 freight cars blown up.

These figures are doubtless subject to the usual discount of Soviet statistics but the Germans themselves have testified to the enormous damage done by guerrillas. As early as September 1942, Hitler himself publicly admitted, "The bands in the East have become an unbearable menace during the last few months, and are seriously threatening the supply lines to the front."

When one recalls that many of the guerrillas who inflicted these damages were potential recruits for Hitler's forces who might have been used not only to supplement the German army but also to carry out diversionary operations in the Soviet rear, one appreciates the twofold handicap Hitler imposed upon his own generals by his political folly.

Early in the war, his experts on Russian affairs and his generals had urged him to permit the formation of Russian units recruited from prisoners and defectors. Not until after his first serious setbacks did he finally consent. But then he circumscribed the use of these "Vlassov troops" so heavily that in the end they contributed little to the German war effort.

Quite aside from Hitler's costly political aberrations, his dismissal of the guerrilla threat at the start of his invasion illustrates his fundamental misunderstanding of irregular warfare which resulted in his sending his troops into Russia without any basic preparation or training for *Kleinkrieg,* or "little war," as the Germans call it.

The ingrained predilection of the German for order even in war renders him peculiarly vulnerable to the disorderliness of irregular combat which he finds not only repugnant but unnerving. Captured letters of German soldiers to their families frequently mentioned the terrifying experience of operating in guerrilla-infested territories far from the combat area where a concealed sniper's bullet might strike them or a mine or grenade blow them sky high.

To the extent that it takes a guerrilla to fight a guerrilla, the German soldier's training was also woefully inadequate. Accustomed to operating in well-organized, compact units with a well-defined channel of command, Hitler's troops were lost when they found themselves operating individually or in small units cut off from their superiors and forced to make their decisions independently. Improvisation, expediency and personal initiative were not on the orderly Prussian curriculum.

To overcome this deficiency, German commanders subsequently sought to form "Hunting Commands" for their "anti-bandit" warfare, recruited from foresters, game wardens and hunters who were accustomed to stalking their quarry alone in silent forests. But even these soon learned that stalking the most elusive old stag was far different from pursuing a wily peasant armed with a rifle.

Not until 1944, five years after the war had started, did the methodical German General Staff produce a training manual which prescribed effective tactics for coping with guerrillas. But it was too late for the German army. Precisely one year after the pamphlet was issued, the German armies surrendered.

The Soviet Partisan movement differed fundamentally from guerrilla movements discussed in previous chapters. The Cuban guerrilla theoretician, Che Guevara, defines this difference thus:

"For the proper analysis of guerrilla warfare it should be noted that there are two different types: first, guerrillas supplement the effort of a large regular army as in the case of the Ukrainian guerrillas; second, an armed group is fighting against an established government."

Much has been written on the activities of the Soviet Partisans during the war, both by Russians and by Germans. Most of the Russian literature deals with the fanatical heroism of the Partisans and their extraordinary exploits which, when checked with German sources, appear to contain a considerable admixture of hyperbole and exaggeration. The Soviet handbook for Partisans, which deals with the techniques of irregular warfare, contains relatively little original material although some of the wiles and stratagems it recommends reflect the Russian genius for improvisation and the cunning and shrewdness of the Russian peasant.

German literature is not much more productive. The manual for anti-Partisan operations previously referred to is singularly devoid of imagination and recommends measures and tactics familiar not only to students of military tactics but to every German hunter of hares or partridges.

During the course of the war, the Russians did, to be sure, develop techniques of radio communication and airborne supply and parachute operations unknown in previous wars. However, the British, and to a certain extent the Americans, had already developed even more sophisticated methods, and, when the Russians undertook to help supply the Partisans in Yugoslavia, their techniques compared to those of the Western Allies could at best be described as rough and ready or, more accurately, simply as primitive.

In one respect, however, the Soviet Partisan movement revealed a significant innovation—its complete organizational separation from the regular military establishment. During the Russian civil war, Partisan detachments had played a role but an insignificant one compared to the conventional units formed after the Bolshevik uprising. But thereafter Partisan warfare seems to have been ignored by the Soviet military and only occasionally mentioned by political ideologists endeavoring to emphasize the role of the masses in future armed conflicts. So far as is known now, when the war broke out in 1941 neither the military establishment nor the Kremlin had made any prior preparations for Partisan operations.

When, immediately after the German invasion began, the political and economic necessity of a Partisan movement became apparent and Stalin, in his plea for a defense of Mother Russia, called upon the citizenry in the path of the enemy advance or already behind enemy lines to destroy their communications and "bring all their measures to nought," he did not assign supervision or co-ordination of the Partisan movement to the armed forces. On the contrary, he turned it over to his political machine, the Communist Party.

On the field level, some senior officers who had joined the Partisans when their units had been overrun did command some Partisan detachments. But as far as is known, no senior officers were ever sent to command even the larger Partisan units.

A directive issued in the first weeks of the war by the White Russian Party Executive Committee on the organization of Partisan bands specifies: "The units are led by unit leaders who are selected by the competent councils from the officers' reserves of the Red Army or from comrades having military training as well as from political leaders and from political organizations. . . ." In practice, however, according to an official Soviet source: "In most cases the leadership of the guerrillas is taken by the secretary of the local Bolshevik Party committee or the president or a member of the board of a collective farm."

According to German sources, political commissars, the Party's ideological police force, were even more heavily represented among the Partisans than in the army itself. In fact, every unit down to the smallest band appeared to have either a political officer or noncom watching over its loyalty. As the operations around Vitebsk related above suggest, there was considerable cooperation between Partisan detachments and Red Army units across the lines but there appears to have been no formal channel of command between the detachments and the Red Army. Partisan operational orders came from the Regional Central Committees of the Party.

The separation of the regulars from the Partisans is even more striking at the top of the command structure in the State Committee for Defense, whose chief was none other than Josef Stalin. The Committee gave orders directly to the Army through the Commissariat for Defense on the one hand and to the Partisans through a separate "Central Staff of the Partisan Movement" on the other. As if to stress even more the complete divorce between the Partisans and the military, the Chief of the Central Staff of the Partisans appointed by Stalin was Pantoleymon K. Ponomarenko, an official of the Party Central Committee, whose sole military experience was as a draftee in the early thirties, since when he had been employed practically exclusively in the Party apparatus. (After the war Ponomarenko continued his political career which ended, publicly at least, as ambassador to the Hague.) Placing the entire operation under civilian Party control would seem to indicate the relatively minor role Stalin attributed to the military aspects of Partisan warfare and the importance he attached to its political aspects. The undeniable successes acknowledged even by Germans of the Partisan movement despite its improvised beginnings would seem to justify his decision.

Current military doctrine in Washington seems to confine the role of American forces in offensive guerrilla operations (as opposed to defensive counterinsurgent operations) to the auxiliary type of warfare typified by the Russian Partisans as an adjunct of conventional warfare. Whether, in the event of nuclear catastrophe, independent guerrilla war without conventional forces might become necessary is a matter of pure speculation.

However, advocates of unconventional operations have urged that in the event of Soviet aggression, guerrilla units either left behind or reinfiltrated into areas overrun by Soviet troops would be extremely useful. This is particularly true since the areas thus overrun would presumably provide the political climate—or as Mao Tse-tung put it, the right temperature—for enlisting a considerable proportion of the population in its support.

While military authorities are not inclined to dispute this argument, some of them point out that in areas where Soviet advances are most likely to occur, namely western Europe, the terrain is singularly unsuited to guerrilla operations because of the density of population and the absence of large inaccessible areas.

This raises the further question of whether useful guerrilla operations must be confined, as Mao Tse-tung suggests, to countries with large uninhabited areas or whether they can be undertaken in urban communities. This question would seem to be worth at least a brief examination.

x Urban Guerrillas

J ULY 26, 1944, was a day long to be remembered by the inhabitants of Warsaw, the Poles and the German occupiers alike. On that day, for the first time since the Germans had captured the capital in 1939, the sound of heavy artillery could be heard in the east. The Poles after five years of occupation pondered the prospect of being liberated by their Russian neighbors with mixed feelings. The Germans patrolling the streets looked ahead to the impending battle for Warsaw with ill-concealed apprehension.

In the headquarters of the Polish Underground Movement, the Commander of the Home Army, General Bor-Komorowski, discussed the impending clash with the local underground politicians in the "home" Parliament. Ever since the Polish capitulation he had been preparing for the coming events methodically and cautiously. Nearly 40,000 men and some 4000 women under his command were awaiting orders to start the hostilities for which he had been training them, planning, caching arms and improvising systems of communications and supply throughout the city.

That morning he had finally received a radio message from the Polish Government in exile in London authorizing him to commence the battle whenever he and the "home" Parliament saw fit. Timing was crucial. The underground army had supplies and arms sufficient only for a week or ten days of fighting at the most. To complicate matters, the exile government had failed to re-establish relations with the Soviet government so that there was no official channel for co-ordinating the planned uprising with the advancing Soviet armies. Repeated attempts to contact the Russian generals in the field by radio and messenger had failed.

Intensely suspicious of the Soviet intentions, the political leaders in the Warsaw underground were determined that the city be in Polish hands and under Polish administration when the Soviet armies entered it. Otherwise, they were convinced the Russian troops would establish their own administration and man it with their own local stooges, the handful of Polish Communists who had until now stubbornly refused to cooperate with Bor-Komorowski's Home Army.

Sternly the politicians told Bor-Komorowski that they would need a minimum of twelve hours after the flight of the Germans to set up their administration and be in a position to meet the entering Russian armies in the capacity of hosts.

Bor-Komorowski promised to fulfill these conditions if he could and returned to his study of the reports of his own intelligence service on the advance of the Russians. A day or two later, six airfields around Warsaw were reported in Soviet hands, the nearest only twenty minutes' flight away. Obviously the Russians were building up for the final assault. But when would it be launched? Once more he tried to get in touch with the Russians through the Communist underground but to his dismay he discovered that the latter had all fled.

Then at 8:15 P.M. on July 29, Moscow radio called upon the

people of Warsaw to rise and carry on an active struggle in the streets against the occupiers. A Soviet manifesto announced: "The Poles to Arms!"

Next day, while he waited uneasily, Bor-Komorowski learned that the Russians had broken through the German outer defenses of the city and that their patrols were only ten miles from the center. On July 31, the Germans themselves announced that the battle for Warsaw had begun. At five P.M. the eastern suburbs were already in Soviet hands.

At last Bor-Komorowski decided the moment had come. The political leaders, summoned in haste, concurred and orders went out that the uprising would commence at five P.M. the next day, August 1.

Though rain was falling next morning the streets were full of Poles seemingly going to their work as usual but actually assembling in their carefully planned mobilization points. Then one by one they fanned out to strategic points in the city: important buildings, central crossroads, key positions overlooking the German barracks and German headquarters, the railroad yards and several factories where arms had been secretly hidden. At each place the first man would ring the doorbell and tell the occupants that the building had been "requisitioned." Then his men would slip in and go to the roofs and windows and balconies covering the key points.

Bor-Komorowski himself left his secret dwelling and moved to the building where his operational headquarters were to be and where radios had been set up to direct the battle. At 4:30 in the afternoon, the Germans suddenly seemed to be re-enforcing the guard of a factory which held a key place in Bor's plans. Fighting broke out and shots were fired but at first the German command dismissed these as "stupid shootings" by lone Polish troublemakers.

But then a truck full of German police was destroyed by a

grenade thrown from a rooftop. At five P.M., as Bor had ordered, the general uprising broke out throughout the city and the Germans were caught off guard. Fifteen minutes later, a general alarm was sounded and German tanks began to move into the center of the city. But maneuvering in the narrow streets they were no match for the Polish fighters, who quickly disabled them with bottles of gasoline hurled from strategic rooftops.

From the start, Bor's greatest problem was communications. Just as the fighting began, the radio transmitter at his headquarters was hit and remained out of commission for hours. German patrols commanded the streets and denied them to the Home Army's messengers, many of whom were young women. By dynamiting the walls between the cellars of buildings, the Poles were able to establish a number of routes which avoided the open streets. Attic walls were likewise broken through and the rooftops themselves at first furnished quick access from one point to another.

But one by one the Germans managed to destroy these underground routes. Then as the Jews had done during the battle of Warsaw's ghetto in 1943, Bor's messengers took to the sewers. Well supplied with detailed maps of the sewage system, they were able to re-establish communications among the various centers of resistance. Sometimes crawling on their stomachs through the filth, sometimes swimming, sometimes clambering up slimy stone waterfalls of sewage, the men and girls of the underground managed to carry messages, supplies, ammunition and even their wounded from one strong point to another. But then the Germans caught on to this expedient too and began dropping grenades and gas bombs down manholes and finally succeeded in closing off most of the sewer routes.

Meanwhile, Bor waited anxiously for the final Russian assault which would divert the German garrison from its battle against the Home Army.

But back in the Kremlin, Stalin had made other plans. Fully aware of the Home Army's purposes, he had no intention of letting the forces of the Polish government-in-exile get credit for liberating Warsaw. Less still did he intend to permit the Polish forces to set up their own government certain to be dominated by non-Communists independent of the "advice" of the Party Commissars, who were near the front waiting to organize the city along Communist lines. Nor was he prepared to negotiate with the Home Army which he rightly suspected was strongly anti-Russian because of the part the Soviet Union had played in the partition of Poland in 1939.

Since he had long known that Bor-Komorowski's army was poised to attack the German occupiers, it was far simpler to let it do so—and be annihilated in the process. Just to be certain it committed suicide, he broadcast his manifesto calling upon the Home Army to take up arms and then ordered his marshals to wait until the Germans had destroyed it.

When word of the uprising reached Hitler, he at once dispatched one of his ablest generals to take command and simultaneously ordered the reserve divisions, which had been awaiting the coming Russian assault, into the city. Overwhelmed by these superior forces, Bor's troops were driven into a handful of strongpoints. In vain their commander pleaded with the Russians by radio to launch their assaults. His messages were not even acknowledged. When his government in London asked the British and American air forces to drop desperately needed ammunition and supplies by parachute, the Western Allies pointed out that they could not lay on sorties all the way to Warsaw without refueling behind the Russian lines. But this Stalin flatly refused.

Nevertheless, the Home Army continued to fight. Bor, as we have noted, had reckoned on a battle of seven days, a maximum of ten. When he realized he had been betrayed by the Soviets he pleaded with his troops to conserve their ammunition. But scattered in their strongholds throughout the capital it was impossible, he said later, to impose such discipline on them.

Gradually their reserves dwindled. Ten days passed but still they fought on. Then twenty days and finally thirty. At last, on September 4, thirty-five days after he had ordered the uprising, all resistance ended. The Home Army had ceased to exist. Then and only then Stalin ordered his marshals to resume their advance.

Doubtless the Poles were unwise to have expected less brutal treatment from the old despot in the Kremlin. But the average human mind, no matter how shrewd, balks at the contemplation of such inhuman treachery and refuses to accept it. The fact remains that Stalin's stratagem was successful and a few days later he was able to install not just a Warsaw government but a so-called Polish government of his own choosing.

But this is not what concerns us here. Contrary to the views of many specialists in unconventional warfare, including Mao Tsetung, who wrote that guerrilla wars were impossible in small countries like Belgium, Bor's thirty-five-day battle with the Germans suggests that unconventional urban warfare operations are by no means impossible. In more recent times, the terror in Algiers and Oran points to the same conclusion. The short lives of the abortive Berlin and Budapest uprisings were due not so much to the unsuitability of the terrain as to the absence of any advance preparation or outside support.

It goes without saying that an urban uprising that does not enjoy outside support will fail against determined opposition. But this does not preclude the possibility of successful guerrilla operations of other kinds in built-up areas.

Perhaps one reason for dismissing the possibility of urban guerrilla operations is that the very word "guerrilla" is generally associated with the wilderness, the mountains of northern Spain, the jungles of Southeast Asia, the plains of China or the deserts of Arabia where bands can hide in caves, dense forests or simply in the vast desert spaces. Guerrillas themselves suggest swift-moving bands in narrow tracks through dense overgrowth, on unknown paths in remote mountain areas or unmapped byways in rural communities.

The guerrilla himself is usually envisaged as a Robin Hood living off the land in the green forest. His skills are those of the stalker: stealthy, soundless movement; a quick eye; an intimate knowledge of the ways of wild animals; the art of camouflage with natural foliage—in short, the city boy's conception of Tarzan.

But as the Polish Home Army discovered, a great city too can provide hidden paths through alleys and cellars, attics and rooftops, just as inaccessible to strangers as a hidden jungle trail. The labyrinthine sewer system of Warsaw may not smell as sweet as a forest path but for a time at least it provided the Polish patriots with a highly effective system of communications.

Every fugitive knows the safety in numbers and few who seek to escape notice seek refuge in the wilderness. Instead they lose themselves in crowds in populated areas. They rely on their knowledge of the ways of man, not of the beast, to escape detection.

As the survivors of the Warsaw uprising also discovered, the ruins of bombed houses provide innumerable half-buried cellars to serve as refuges and bases. For the counterinsurgent, as the generals of World War II learned, no terrain is less accessible to tanks than a bombed-out city whose streets are piled high in rubble and lined with burned-out buildings, providing ideal hideouts for guerrillas armed with snipers' guns and grenades.

As the Malayan Communists found out, conventional guerrillas operating in the jungle or in the desert are vitally dependent on supplies from elsewhere. The urban guerrilla, on the other hand, operates in the very heart of the supply system. Not only food markets but pharmacies with their medicines and workshops for the repair of arms and manufacture of bombs and other weapons are readily available.

Nevertheless, the urban guerrilla operates under many disadvantages unknown to the rural guerrilla, which limit the kinds of operations he can undertake. The assembly of large numbers of men and their redispersal after a strike in force is well nigh impossible under the eyes of a vigilant police. The risk of recognition even in a crowd by informers requires a much more sophisticated security system than in the case of rural guerrillas.

Hence, until they undertake an all-out strike like the Warsaw uprising, urban guerrillas must confine themselves to operations which can be carried out in small numbers and avoid all risks of open street fights in which the rebels can be identified. Yet even in this respect they enjoy some advantages over rural guerrillas. Because they are in the heart of a communications center, which ordinarily houses the headquarters of large enemy forces, their opportunities for intelligence gathering are greatly increased. Furthermore, the communications center itself is more vulnerable to damage than the individual rail or telegraph lines stretching through a rural area. The sabotage of a marshaling yard, for example, can damage the enemy more severely than the blowing up of a culvert on a single line. The destruction of a telegraph or telephone center can cripple the enemy far more than cutting an individual wire. While the urban guerrilla can seldom ambush and annihilate enemy patrols, he has far better opportunities in a headquarters town to liquidate key enemy personnel as they travel through its confined streets.

Finally, guerrillas operating in densely populated areas, where the level of education is normally much higher than in remote villages, have a greater opportunity to carry on their propaganda and recruiting. From the scrawling of antienemy slogans on walls, to the distribution of pamphlets and posters and the holding of secret meetings, they are in a much better position to instill their ideas in the masses than the guerrilla operating among semi-literate or illiterate peasants.

The skills of the urban guerrilla are as different from those of his rural colleague as the skills of an office clerk or a factory worker are from those of the woodsman or peasant. Though he must be as familiar with the alleys and cellars, the sewers and utility tunnels of his town as the rural fighter is with his mountain tracks and forest trails, he must seek concealment not under a hat covered with native foliage but in his ability for dissimulation—being a peaceful electrician by day and a skilled saboteur of telephone switchboards and radio transmitters by night. Instead of being able to ambush enemy convoys he must know the tricks of sabotaging the enemy's vehicles standing in their garages and motor pools, pouring graphite into their transmissions and sugar in their tanks instead of laying mines on roads and blowing up culverts.

It need hardly be pointed out that as the industrial revolution penetrates into the rural areas, these are the skills that are rapidly replacing the nature lore and the woodsman's arts. In America and Europe today, even the farmer is becoming more skilled in maintaining a tractor than in caring for a sick horse, more familiar with the power saw than the axe, more at home on the highway than in the trackless forest.

The tendency of respected military authorities to dismiss the possibilities of guerrilla warfare in thickly populated areas such as western Europe is understandable. The more respectable they are the more repugnant the unconventional methods and unchivalrous ethics of guerrillas appear to them even in rural areas. Since the methods of urban guerrillas must be even more unconventional and their ethics even less chivalrous with their greater emphasis on assassination and terror, the mere contemplation of such operations is the more abhorrent.

But to ignore the possibility of future guerrilla operations in thickly populated areas and to fail to provide adequate training and preparation to carry it out or to counteract it would seem to be almost as shortsighted as Hitler's dismissal of the guerrilla problem in Russia with the order to "liquidate them ruthlessly in combat or while trying to escape."

XI Latin America

IN AFRICA and the Near East, particularly in Iran and the Arabian peninsula, potential guerrilla movements are developing. Nearer to home, Latin America seethes with grievances, political rivalries, feuds and frustrated national or racial aspirations which are the lifeblood of guerrillas. As recently as February 1963, President Kennedy, addressing himself to the threat of Castro's subversive activities abroad, stated: "I think the big dangers to Latin America . . . are the very difficult and in some cases desperate conditions in the countries themselves, unrelated to Cuba: illiteracy or bad housing, mal-distribution of wealth or political or social instability. . . . It is the desperate and in some cases internal problems in Latin America . . . which cause me the concern and why I regard Latin America as the most critical area in the world today."

In the past the *coup d'état*—a primitive form of insurgency—has been an established political tradition in Latin America where rivals for power have been confined to a thin stratum of the political elite. But today the rivalries are penetrating to the lowest economic and social levels; and racial groupings and the systematic efforts of the Communist Party to foster, exploit and capture incipient insurgent movements based on the discontents and grievances of the less privileged no longer permit us to dismiss the *coup d'état* as a somewhat comical aspect of Latin American political life. The Communist system not only has perfected a technique for retaining power once seized; it also has a built-in tendency to expand and to prostitute itself to the interests of the most powerful empire that has yet threatened our country.

While Cuba has illustrated both these tendencies, it would be misleading to overestimate its role as a source of subversive insurgent operations. It has neither the financial nor material resources to serve as more than a staging area for insurgent operations, and ideologically, as President Kennedy has pointed out, its escutcheon as the shield bearer of Socialist revolution has been badly tarnished by its humiliation both by the United States and the Soviet Union.

Nevertheless, regardless of Cuba, the emergence of Communism in Latin America has saddled the United States with a dual obligation: We must perfect our capabilities and those of our Latin neighbors in the art of counterinsurgency, and—because of the possibility of a sudden *coup d'état* or the capture of a reform movement by the Communists, as in Guatemala and Cuba—we must develop our capacity to launch where necessary an active guerrilla operation against an established Communist dictatorship. This latter capability is enormously complicated by the traditional dislike of the Yankee in Latin America and, paradoxically, by our own sympathies for antifeudal reform elements which, if captured by the Communists, may well turn up across the barricades from our own forces.

A cursory glance at almost any Latin American country will reveal the grievances, rivalries and social injustices that cause President Kennedy such grave concern. Scarcely a single country-desk head in the State Department's Bureau of Inter-American Affairs does not jealously claim critical status for the country under his surveillance. At the risk of offending the majority of them, let us take a brief look at only five.

A few hundred miles south of the border the Republic of Guatemala has for decades seethed with political discontent. The instability of its political structure is emphasized by two circumstances. Almost two thirds of its population is Indian and therefore beyond the pale of political activity. Secondly, it has already experienced a revolution which has whetted its appetite for social reform.

The one third of the population that is politically active is composed of a landed gentry, re-enforced in recent times by a newly arrived commercial and financial class, and—opposing the conservatism of these groups—the intellectuals, the doctors, writers, journalists and professional men, supported by a politically immature but active and very vocal university student body. Dividing its allegiance between the two is a somewhat ludicrous and highly unreliable army, one third of whose officers hold the top rank of colonel.

There is little that is original about the issues dividing the Right from the Left: the mal-distribution of political power, economic wealth and land. The poverty of the rural workers has, as elsewhere in Latin America, driven hundreds of thousands to the cities, where they live in squalor and idleness. Illiteracy is among the highest in Central America, about sixty-five per cent, thus condemning two thirds of the country to frustrated inferiority.

The landed gentry and the newly rich commercial class are by and large content with the status quo and vigorously oppose any reforms, social or economic. The Left, whose appetite has been stirred but not satisfied by the revolution of 1944–54, advocates either Communism or varying degrees of Socialism. An added element of controversy is the economic power of the United Fruit

Company which is constantly accused of exploiting the country for foreign interests.

Currently, the Right, supported by the army, is in power but elections have been promised for late in 1963. The leading Leftist, Juan José Arévalo, presently in exile, threatens to run and since he is highly popular among the reform element his chances of success are high. But because he once delivered his movement into the hands of the Communists under President Arbenz, the Rightist and conservative elements in the army are determined to forestall his election, either by preventing his candidacy or by postponing the elections. In either case the Left threatens to strike for power. Thus, to prevent a Communist take-over, the United States is faced with the equally obnoxious alternatives of supporting the feudal right to retain power or, if the extreme Left gains power, of encouraging an insurgent movement to oust it.

A thousand miles further south in Peru we find another overwhelming majority of Indians not only excluded from national politics but often living in actual peonage or slavery on the estates of absentee landlords high in the Andes. Again rising population pressures have forced hundreds of thousands to cluster in the suburbs of Lima in settlements which even the police do not dare enter and which are powder kegs of unrest and discontent. Again illiteracy, inadequate housing and unemployment are grievances which the Communists have for years sought to exploit, thus far without success.

From June 1962–1963 a military junta ruled the country, though the APRA party* under the strongly anti-Communist Haya de la Torre was expected to win the next election. To oppose it and its reform program, the Rightist oligarchy with military support was prepared to go to any length, including, if necessary, cooperation with the Communist Left. But, as it turned out, the election was won by Fernando Belaúnde Terry,

* People's Party.

leader of the left-wing Popular Action party, the man who had been considered least likely to succeed.

The army itself is divided among conservatives and progressive-minded younger officers. University students have in the past been strongly Communist, but recently anti-Communist student organizations have been gaining the upper hand.

In the mountains, the Indians goaded by poverty and the greed of absentee landlords are stirring restlessly. Should a conflict arise in the center, the possibility that the once inert Indian population will take part, either under Communist leadership or independently, cannot be excluded. Fortunately the Communist organization is itself in disarray, split between numerous factions. Nevertheless, if the balloon goes up in Peru we are apt to be confronted with a long and bitter struggle from which it will be difficult to stand aloof unless we are willing to risk a Communist take-over by default.

Next door to Peru, Bolivia, like Guatemala, has already tasted the heady wine of revolution a decade ago and as in Guatemala its appetite has grown with eating. The eighty per cent Indian population has to a limited extent been integrated into the national life and has acquired aspirations of its own through its seizure of many landed estates in the hinterland. The army, discredited by the revolution, has been replaced as the leading force by a dual militia made up of organized tin mine laborers on the one hand and a peasant or Indian militia on the other.

The present MNR government* is split between a moderate center and a radical Left under the effective leadership of Juan Lechin O. Quendo. Lechin is supported by the labor militia and at least up till now the moderates have been able to count on the peasant militia.

No country in Latin America has a more difficult economic problem. On the one hand its nationalized tin mine industry, dominated by organized labor, is inefficient and burdened with

* Nationalist Revolutionary Movement.

featherbedding. Its attempts to diversify its economy by encouraging cattle raising, sugar, oil and other industries in the lowlands have been paralyzed by the refusal of Indians to come down from their mountain villages to work in the lowlands. As a result the per capita income in Bolivia is the lowest in Latin America.

Further north, just south of the Panama Canal, Colombia has long been regarded as one of the most hopeful of the countries of South America. It has no Indian problem to speak of. Between 1908 and 1948 it established a tradition of stable, democratic government in which a conservative and a liberal party competed more or less peacefully for power. Its coffee economy has sought greater stability by a program of diversification. Its ruling elements are on the whole well educated and extremely patriotic.

But beneath this apparent stability lie the seeds if not the deep roots of violent rivalries and dissension. Within a hundred miles or so of Bogotá the government writ ceases to run. In the rugged areas where communications are deplorable village caudillos or headmen run their little domains like feudal barons. Some of them consider themselves "conservatives," others proudly display their "liberal" colors and whenever the two meet there is apt to be fighting and bloodshed. This feuding has often been compared to the squabbles that have prevailed among the feuding families in the mountains of Kentucky and Tennessee. Though some of the rivalry has its origin in political differences, ideology has ceased to be a real source of contention except in two areas where the local caudillos subscribe to Communist doctrine—in Viotá and Sumapaz which occasionally provide asylum to Communist fugitives from the coastal areas.

Basically, the grievances that tear the country apart are those of other Latin American countries—mal-distribution of wealth and of land. In some areas, the visitor finds broad fertile valleys owned by absentee landlords and used largely for grazing, while on the barren, eroded hillsides above, peasants grow coffee on tiny parcels of land which seldom provide subsistence for their owners. Rural housing is generally deplorable and rural poverty has led to a movement to the cities which has created slums comparable to those on the outskirts of Lima.

As a result of the Rojas Pinella dictatorship between 1948 and 1958, the army is generally distrusted by the rural elements. The ambushing of military units sent to pacify the countryside has been a national pastime providing the rural bandits and village caudillos with captured arms and ammunition to continue their lawless existence. Thus, violence has become a tradition which until now has been motivated largely by a combination of prestige, boredom and economic distress but which could, if properly led, be directed into political channels by extreme Leftists.

This danger is well recognized by the regime which in recent times has joined with the Catholic Church in a campaign of pacification. The campaign is a two-pronged one involving in the first instance a rural education and vocational training program conducted by radio, the building of roads, medical and economic assistance for the poverty-stricken villagers, and on the other hand, a tough military campaign carried out by guerrilla-trained commandos known as hunter-killer squads which are attempting to suppress the feuding bandits and caudillos.

Currently the government rests on an uneasy coalition between the conservatives and the liberals who alternately elect the president. Few experts dare predict how long this artificial partnership will last. Meantime extreme Left-wing groups are doing their best to exploit the country's unrest and to harness the lawless elements to their Communist bandwagon.

Next door to Colombia, Venezuela presents perhaps the most glaring contrast between extreme wealth and utter poverty. Here they exist side by side in a tense, uneasy truce which, as during Vice-President Nixon's visit, occasionally explodes into angry demonstrations. In Caracas, palatial mansions, luxurious hotels and other conspicuous symbols of oil-based wealth stand almost cheek by jowl with squalid slums inhabited by unemployed or semi-employed proletarians who provide heavy support for the country's extreme Left politicians. In the countryside, though the peasantry is poor, it has recently benefited from progressive land-reforms and housing measures and tends to be less radical.

The present government of President Betancourt, though Left of center, has the distinction of being the only civilian-elected government to last a full constitutional term. While Betancourt enjoys the support of the peasantry he is violently opposed by the extreme Left-wing urban population under varied leadership. He is equally violently opposed by all elements Right of center, including most of the wealthy oil and industrial interests, and thus manages to survive on a narrow strip of moderate Left-wing backing.

The military, once the traditional arbiter, is itself in disarray. Some officers tend to support Betancourt while the rest, more conservative, watch his government with a suspicious eye, ready to step in if in their view he veers too far from his position.

The Communist Party, including Castro's supporters and others who pay allegiance to the Peking school, is exceedingly active both among the university students and the urban proletariat. In recent months it has attempted to extend its influence to the rural working class but without much success. When a Castro-ite young journalist recently took to the hills to raise the peasantry against the government, he was promptly seized by pro-Betancourt farmers and turned over to the authorities and is currently languishing in a Caracas jail.

The familiar grievances which wrack the country are aggravated by Venezuela's dependence on its oil exports. Lacking almost all other industries, it relies on imports, largely from the United States, for most of its consumer goods. And from this dependence springs the traditional animosity toward Yankee imperialism, ably exploited by the extreme Left.

Thus far, Betancourt has by means of his agrarian and housing reforms miraculously and unprecedentedly managed to walk the tightrope between the powerful oligarchy of wealth and the rest-

less mobs of unemployed in the urban slums. Because of his reforms he has managed to forestall extreme Left-wing efforts to
use the radical mobs to throw him out. The anti-Communist
Right has likewise hesitated to oust him with military force, lest
by so doing it drive the entire Left of center element both in the
cities and the countryside into the arms of the extremist, pro-
Castro leaders.

One could easily continue down the roster of Latin American
states and almost without exception discover deep-seated grievances and dissatisfactions which in recent years have stirred the
people against the traditional feudal oligarchies which have ruled
them since the Spaniards departed. Illiteracy, racial discrimina-
tion against the Indian, intellectual ferment among students,
urbanization and a growing proletariat, lack of economic opportunity for a burgeoning population, to say nothing of the economic ills of a continent dependent on the export of a few raw
materials for their essential imports—any one of these could provide an able, resolute leader with all the slogans and panaceas a
guerrilla could ask for to start an insurgent uprising. In fact they
have all been used before to overthrow unpopular regimes and
establish transient popular governments. But today, because of
the techniques and support available from the Communist world,
such uprisings are apt to be permanent.

Where once it was a diplomatic convenience to be able to deal
with such movements deftly, usually successfully and occasionally
even tactfully, today it has become an imperative to develop the
understanding and capacity to prevent the permanent subversion
of an entire continent at our doorstep. We must not only be able
to detect the first signs of such a movement but we must have
ready for instant use the means of dealing with it, of locating its
vital center, impeding its driving force, diverting its clandestine
thrusts—and finally isolating and destroying it.

XII Conclusions

IT WOULD BE almost superfluous at this point to return to the sad story of the Bay of Pigs and apply to it the lessons provided by the cases examined in the previous chapters. In the final stage as executed, that landing was a most uninspired, conventional military operation—a miniature invasion modeled on the first phase of amphibious operations of World War II but without the follow-through. The only unconventional feature of it was the invading force.

But if we go back to the early planning stage, when the question first arose of eliminating Castro by force, the relevancy of these lessons becomes more apparent. We can presume that from the outset, for sound political reasons, the idea of using large American forces for the task was rejected. Thus the problem was reduced to how best to employ an improvised army of exiles to do the job. Simple arithmetic showed that the initial combat force could be only a fraction of the Cuban army. On the other hand, political estimates indicated that the potential support among the mass of Cubans was considerable. Thus it required no intensive study of T. E. Lawrence or Mao Tse-tung to appreciate that an unconventional operation was called for. Indeed this was the original concept.

Once this fact was established, it would appear only logical to have applied the basic criteria of unconventional operations and to plan a campaign based on them. The first step would have been to formulate a genuine political program to rally the potential support of the islanders—not just the elimination of Castro and after that, to quote one of the planners, "inevitable chaos." The second step would have been to provide a genuine, united leadership—not an incohesive front of widely disparate political groups. The third step would have been to prepare the local ground prior to the combat phase and to lay plans for the gradual development of the movement from necessarily tiny units to the force necessary to challenge Castro's army.

Other steps would have included the establishment of island bases in which to assemble recruits and channels to the internal opposition to prevent the movement's isolation and, not least, the indoctrination of the recruits to provide the essential discipline and security on which such a movement is dependent.

But instead, quite another approach was taken, partly perhaps owing to the lack of time due to the rapidly growing efficiency of Castro's security police; partly because of the expected increase in Castro's air power (though this could hardly have affected a guerrilla operation) but partly, it seems to me, because of a decision by the planners that this was primarily a military operation and that military experts applying military considerations should decide how the available forces were to be used.

This preoccupation with the military aspects and the predominance given to them was demonstrated when, just before the decision to go ahead was given, the highest military experts in the government were called upon to give the final judgment on whether the operation was militarily sound. (Ostensibly for security reasons, no such judgment was asked of the political experts dealing with Cuba in the State Department.)

While the Bay of Pigs revealed a less than adequate understanding of aggressive guerrilla operations, our actions in Vietnam since 1961 have demonstrated a somewhat better grasp of the principles of defensive, counterinsurgent warfare. In the opening chapter I pointed out that in 1960 a new plan of approach to the situation there was set down in a lengthy document prepared by American political officials in Saigon in collaboration with the Vietnamese and eventually submitted for approval to the Pentagon. Thus when the Kennedy administration came into office in 1961, determined to reinvigorate our efforts in Vietnam, a plan, at least, was ready. But despite the high priorities assigned to its implementation by the new administration, the lead time from blue print to operations was long and costly. New types of weapons had to be assembled, shipped and distributed. Troops had to be taught to use them. American personnel including Special Forces had to be schooled and sent to Saigon. Most important of all, American and Vietnamese officers and officials in Saigon had to be instructed and persuaded to put the novel ideas of the program into operation.

Fortunately for the planners, the Kennedy administration moved with the vigor it has come to symbolize. In the spring of 1961 Vice-President Johnson was sent to Saigon to stimulate Vietnamese cooperation and to try to boost the people's sinking morale. An experienced international economist, Eugene Staley, was dispatched to work out the economic aspects of the program, with special emphasis on aid to rural communities. Later, as the equipment began to roll through the pipe line, General Maxwell Taylor and a staff of military and civilian officials were sent out to inspect progress and to accelerate preparations.

Some parts of the new plan had been put into effect at once in a rather helter-skelter fashion and the first results were under-standably discouraging. This was particularly true of the first attempts to implement Operation Sunrise, which was designed to win over the peasants by protecting them in strategic hamlets but which was initially carried out with such vigor that the dazed and resentful peasants found themselves herded like sheep into compounds that must have looked to them more like concentration camps than the privileged peek into Paradise they were led to expect.

Despite the assurances of Vice-President Johnson and General Taylor, other aspects of the new strategy lagged and did not make sufficient progress to turn the tide of discouragement. By December 1961, morale in and around Saigon among Vietnamese and Americans had reached its lowest point. But then at last the curve flattened out and eventually turned upward.

In essence, the new strategy was an adaptation and combination of Magsaysay's civic action program described in Chapter III and the British isolation tactic in Malaya described in Chapter VII. In fact, a talented and experienced British colonial police official, Mr. Robert K. G. Thompson, who had participated in the Malayan campaign, was invited, albeit with some initial resistance from the American military, to help develop the strategy and eventually contributed very substantially to its implementation.

The need to cut off the guerrillas from the peasantry by fortifying the latter's villages and preventing them from aiding the guerrillas was not new to Diem. As early as 1958 he had worked out a scheme for constructing "agro-villes" into each of which thousands of peasants were to be brought from surrounding villages and hamlets. However, the original plan had bogged down for several reasons. In the first place, the towns designed by somewhat idealistic architects were so elaborate and modern that they were extremely expensive and generally unsuited to the needs of the primitive peasants. For example, each town was cen-

tered about a luxuriant, shady lawn where the architec‌
the peasants might stroll among the palms of a warm e‌
whereas what the peasants needed was a central stockade‌
they could lock up their cattle at night. In the second place‌
cause of the proposed size of the agro-villes it was necessar‌
uproot peasants for miles around and resettle them far from th‌
ancestral fields and rice paddies.

The new plan went to the opposite extreme of fortifying each‌
individual hamlet, the smallest unit of Vietnamese community‌
life, which ordinarily, with two or three other hamlets clustered‌
around a market place, forms the peasant village. These fortified‌
or strategic hamlets were surrounded by barbed wire or in less‌
exposed areas by cactus fences and protected by a home guard‌
recruited from the village itself. Each hamlet was to have a radio‌
transmitter so that in the event of attack by the Vietcong it could‌
summon aid.

The strategic hamlet program was inaugurated in March of‌
1962. At first the selection of hamlets depended more on the‌
individual initiative and energy of provincial and village officials‌
than on a rationally planned schedule. As a result they popped up‌
in haphazard fashion across the countryside, often in locales‌
where they could least be protected or re-enforced in case of Viet-‌
cong attacks. And once again local enthusiasm ran ahead of‌
prudence, and local officials herded bewildered, uncomprehend-‌
ing peasants into stockades, with the result that at the first oppor-‌
tunity the young men took off for the jungle.

While the hamlets were being fortified, the Vietnamese army‌
was undergoing thorough reorganization and retraining in small‌
units suitable for guerrilla operations. Airborne units for helicop-‌
ter battalions were formed, and ranger squads were trained to go‌
out and support themselves for weeks on end in the jungle while‌
they pursued Vietcong bands.

One of the most vital and valuable aspects of the new program was the overhauling of the intelligence system, initiated by General Taylor. In the early days of the war, such information on the movement of Vietcong bands as filtered into headquarters was usually long out of date and thoroughly garbled by repeated relaying and reinterpretation at each stage of transmission. The new program provided for radios for the immediate and direct dispatch of all raw intelligence from the smallest village to the top headquarters where it was assembled and evaluated. To insure accuracy and speed, American military personnel were also assigned to the villages as intelligence advisers to the local authorities.

But even these innovations proved slow in taking effect and many shortcomings were soon revealed. Among them was an old one we have discussed in earlier chapters, particularly in connection with Magsaysay's operations against the Huks—namely, the antagonism which Vietnamese soldiers aroused among the villagers by the troops' often highhanded and arrogant requisitioning and the distrustful hostility engendered by their understandable fear of treachery or ambush.

As a result of these and other shortcomings the program was revised in 1962. In each province an orderly schedule of priorities for the fortification of villages was established, based not on haphazard availability but on the tactical principle that strategic hamlets should be located in fan-shaped fashion radiating from the more secure to less secure areas, so that they could not only provide mutual protection but also be more easily re-enforced from the center.

At the same time a co-ordinated American program was organized under the supervision of the seconds in command among the diplomatic and military personnel in Saigon known as the "countryside team," which was to provide personnel and supplies for civic action in the villages. Medical, economic, engineering, agricultural and sanitation personnel were dispatched to the rural areas equipped with tools, medicines, seeds and even breeding livestock to help the peasants re-establish their war-torn villages.

Even this program ran into unexpected problems. For example, one of the most desperately needed items in the villages was rat poison, so the civic action teams came fully equipped with the most modern type, guaranteed to kill rats but harmless for babies, pigs and other non-vermin. The Vietnamese farmers, however, had become accustomed during the French regime to using a certain type of French rat poison which, while it killed rats, was equally effective against livestock and humans. The civic action teams argued that their rat poison was far superior to the French rat poison. The peasants were unconvinced. In the end, after lengthy financial manipulations, French rat poison was imported from France and the peasants, but perhaps not their pigs, were happy.

In many respects the new program is already scoring a success. Of 16,000 hamlets about one fourth have been fortified and by the end of 1963 much of the countryside will have been cleared and prepared for defense. In 1961 the Vietcong could boast undisputed control of many areas which they used for rest, recuperation, retraining and resupply. These included the notorious Zone D, scarcely sixty miles north of Saigon, and the equally infested marshlands of an Xuyen province in the southwest known as the Duong Minh Chau area. Today, American officials claim there is not a single area in the country which Vietnamese rangers cannot penetrate at will. While the Vietcong still maintain hidden base camps they are no longer permanent and none of them are immune from raids by government troops.

In recent encounters between the Vietcong and the Vietnamese regulars, the ratio of weapons captured to weapons lost has shifted from two to one in favor of the Vietcong to four to three in favor of the Vietnamese. Captured documents indicate that for the first time the Vietcong are running increasingly short of food and medicine. Defectors from the Communist camp who in 1962 were surrendering at the rate of only twenty-five a week are coming in today three times as frequently. The efforts to teach Vietnamese regulars to be nicer to peasants is paying off in better relations in the villages.

The new civic action program coupled with well-co-ordinated propaganda, especially films, is likewise beginning to impress the peasantry. Not only has there been a decrease of incidents involving village aid to the Vietcong but there has been a substantial increase in the amount of information on guerrilla movements flowing from the villages to the Vietnamese headquarters.

Two years ago, Ho Chi Minh, the North Vietnamese Communist leader, predicted that within a year the United States would have lost its appetite for the struggle in Vietnam and like the French would abandon Diem to his fate. Recently he has revised this prophecy and has suggested that the war may continue another twenty or thirty years.

Though American officials both in Saigon and Washington warn that, as in Greece, Malaya and the Philippines, the war against the guerrillas may drag on for many years, they are cautiously suggesting that the tide has turned against the Vietcong. Nineteen sixty-three, they say, is the critical year. If current successes continue, some of them even suggest privately that within five years the guerrillas will have been eliminated.

In only one respect is there serious reason to question this confidence but it is a crucial one—the viability of Diem's regime and its ability to mobilize and lead the native talents necessary to carry the fight through to a finish. Few Americans who know him deny that Diem himself is an autocrat, his regime dictatorial and on the lower levels, at least, notoriously inefficient and even corrupt. The descendant of a family of court officials, a devout Catholic, ascetic and withdrawn, Diem relies for advice practically exclusively on a tiny circle of relatives including his brother

Nhu and his sister-in-law, Mme. Nhu. The Vietnamese Parliament is largely dominated by him and has little real power, though recently Diem has granted it the right to question his cabinet ministers after the fashion of the British Parliament.

Like Lenin, the only place Diem provides for an active opposition is the jail, though he permits his critics the freedom of Saigon's cafés where they spend their days complaining to whoever will listen—usually foreign visitors and journalists. He completely controls the Vietnamese press and keeps a tight rein on military operations. All important provincial authorities are hand picked by him, though he has recently allowed the villages to elect their own spokesmen. Distrustful of all his lieutenants, he does not permit even a centralized intelligence system lest it somehow be used against him.

Personally upright and by local standards a man of high ethics and unquestioned courage, he is nevertheless devoid of the charism which makes a popular leader. Though he travels considerably in the provinces he is not one to inspire warm personal loyalties. In the towns, particularly Saigon, he is detested by the so-called intellectuals who have remained in Vietnam just as he is by the thousands of *émigrés* who have deserted their country for the comforts of Paris. Finally, lacking the tact, the sycophantic finesse and the sophisticated cajolery with which Western governments soothe the egos and sensibilities of the international press, he and particularly his anti-American brother Nhu have alienated most of the foreign journalists who visit Saigon and through them much international public opinion.

Under these circumstances one may well question whether Diem's government is viable. Can it stay the long, bitter course against the guerrillas of Ho Chi Minh? Some Americans and other foreigners even question whether the United States should continue to tolerate him as head of the recognized government. The corruption and inefficiency of his subordinates, especially the tax collectors in the villages, provide ample grist for the Vietcong propaganda mill, and his unpopularity and highhandedness have deprived him of the support of many able Vietnamese sorely needed in the struggle against the Vietminh.

To such critics, his American supporters almost invariably reply that there is no one else who could adequately lead and control the country in its present crisis. While there are some young men in his regime who are learning to shoulder responsibility and who might, in the future, carry on were he removed, at present there is no other strong hand that could keep the regime functioning.

Granted that his system falls far short of the minimum Western standards of democracy, his defenders argue, the people he rules are themselves just as wanting by tradition, training and mentality in the traits required of a citizen of a Western type of democracy. Whatever its defects, they say, his regime is suited to his time and his people.

Diem is himself an ardent believer in education and has made great strides in providing schools for his country's children. In the eight years since he came to power the number of school children has more than doubled and at present there are nearly a million and a half of them—considerably more than in North Vietnam, despite Ho Chi Minh's vaunted educational program. Given time, a new generation better adapted to the needs of a democratic regime may emerge.

Diem's most vocal and bitter critics come from Saigon's intellectual set, though by no means all intellectuals oppose him. Trained by the French and with few national loyalties or patriotic compulsions, they appear content to sit on the sidelines in Saigon or in Paris and jeer at both Diem and his Vietcong adversaries, unwilling to take a hand themselves or even to take sides until they see who will win and then provide them with the sinecures they covet. Fortunately, Diem's supporters point out, the war now being waged in the jungles and swamps of the hinterland is not likely to be decided in the cafés of either Saigon or Paris.

Where it will be decided, as Diem long since recognized, is in the villages and hamlets. It is the peasantry who, in the final analysis, will determine whether the temperature of the water is more favorable for the Vietcong guerrillas or Diem's regulars. For centuries, probably from the time their ancestors settled the country, the peasants have lived completely isolated from the city and the central government. They have had no concept whatever of the nation and to it they have considered they owe no allegiance and only such support as the tax collector can extract from them.

Whether the current strategy can reverse this attitude and forge the essential link between the village and the capital will in the end decide the outcome of this guerrilla war, just as it has determined the outcome of so many other similar wars before it. To one who must rely for his information on reports trickling in from officials and unofficial sources in Saigon, the best guess today is that the Vietcong's once high hopes are waning.

There is little likelihood that a full-grown democracy will spring up from the ruins of France's Asiatic colonial empire. But provided the American taxpayer and his representatives in Congress do not succumb to the battle fatigue which overwhelmed the French, there is an excellent chance that Vietnam can, at least, be saved from the colonizers of the new Communist empire.

To leap from this tentative prediction to the conclusion that the United States has finally mastered the complexities of guerrilla war and proved its capacity to conduct any future counterinsurgent campaign would be the height of folly. In the first place, as I pointed out in the first chapter, it took many precious months, if not years, for the American observers in Vietnam even to recognize the basic nature of the conflict. We have no assurance that other observers in other areas will recognize future challenges before it is too late.

Furthermore the strategy finally adopted in Vietnam was reached only by the most costly trial-and-error method. Nor is it necessarily suitable for dealing with other insurgent operations in other parts of the world.

Finally the policy- and decision-making machinery which now directs the operation with apparent success is entirely fortuitous— a result of the energetic intellectual curiosity of the youthful new administration in Washington and of the equally fortunate personal relationships that have been developed between the political and military representatives in the field in Vietnam. As yet there is no established machinery or even an accepted philosophy to guide us when we are next confronted with a similar threat.

Here, I suggest, we are reaching the very heart of our problem: the American concept or lack of concept of the relationship between warmaking and politics; the idea that when war comes, the generals take over and the political branch meekly steps aside. In Vietnam the politicians stepped—or were pushed—aside before the military on the spot even realized there was a war on.

We have already cited Clausewitz's well-known definition of war as "nothing but a continuation of political intercourse with a mixture of other means." In his voluminous study, he examines in detail the relationship of the political leadership (which he calls "the cabinet") to the military. In evaluating his views, one should remember that Clausewitz was a product of the Prussian military school and a proud member of the Prussian military caste which was notorious for its contempt for its political colleagues in the government. Hence he can scarcely be accused of prejudice in favor of the political branch.

The cabinet alone, Clausewitz asserts, should determine not only the aims of war but also the extent of the effort to be made for its achievement. "To leave a great military enterprise or the plan for one to a purely military judgment and decision is impermissible." It is irrational, he insists, to consult professional soldiers on the plan of a war and solicit from them "a purely military opinion" on what the cabinet ought to do. It is even more absurd, he says, for the political branch "to give the military a statement of available means in order that it should draw up a purely military plan for a war or even for a campaign."

Repeatedly he admonishes that "the subordination of the political point of view to the military would be contrary to common sense." He even goes further and suggests that familiarity with military matters is not the primary qualification of a war minister. Indeed, he suggests that good soldiers as war ministers have often given the worst military advice. "The leading outlines of a war are always determined by the cabinet," he says, "that is, by a political not a military organ."

Clausewitz does not, of course, suggest that "the cabinet" interfere with the detailed execution of military operations or become involved in maneuvers on the field of battle. "The political element does not sink deep in the details of war. Vedettes are not planted, patrols do not make their rounds from political considerations; but small as is its influence in this respect, it is great in the formation of a plan for a whole war or a campaign and often even for a battle."

Interference of the political element in the conduct of war can only be harmful, Clausewitz suggests, if the policy itself is wrong. Thus Hitler's interference in the military operations of the Wehrmacht during World War II was harmful chiefly because his basic policies and his so-called intuition were in themselves at fault. The same has been said of Stalin by his successors.

During the last war, the British seem to have come closest to following Clausewitz' advice that the military should at all times be subordinated to the political branch. Few English generals failed to solicit and follow the advice of the political branch of the government. Churchill himself interfered daily in command decisions to make certain that operations coincided with his political aims.

American practice, however, seems to have ignored Clause-

witz' advice altogether. Fluctuating violently between two ex-
tremes, it has in peacetime, except for Cold War problems,
prohibited any interference of generals in political affairs. In war,
however, it has thrust the political branch aside and given the
generals almost free rein to decide both political and military
questions.

The reason for this attitude can perhaps be explained partly on
historic grounds: the early isolation of the country from the European scene, the fact that the few wars it has fought in modern
times prior to World War I were against relatively weak powers
and the issues relatively simple. Partly, I think, it can be ascribed
to the moral position the American people have taken toward
war. Every war we have undertaken has been pictured as a moral
crusade against the forces of evil rather than for a political advantage. Since there is no compromise between right and wrong,
only complete victory and "unconditional surrender" are considered acceptable.

Though we occasionally tend to attribute both wisdom and
virtue to our successful generals after a war, and even elect some
of them to the highest political office, in peacetime we usually
look upon them with profound suspicion, reflecting a deep-seated
fear of "men on horseback," who might threaten our democratic
institutions. From the moment a new cadet enters the Sallyport
of the Military Academy at West Point until he retires—or a war
breaks out—he is sternly abjured from any political activity or
even from expressing political opinions.

But whatever the causes, there is ample evidence of this contradiction in our attitudes in peacetime and war. During World
War II, when Churchill advanced the strategy of an attack on
Europe's "soft underbelly" with the object of interjecting Western
troops between the advancing Russians and western Europe and
occupying central Europe before the Russians got there, it was
rejected by the United States on the advice of the Joint Chiefs of

Staff on purely military grounds—chiefly logistic. There appears to be no evidence that the political advantages of such a strategy were ever even given a serious hearing.

Throughout the war the Nazi machine was considered by the American command as our primary and only target, one that had to be physically destroyed. Though the political branch was well aware that the Red Army constituted a hardly less dangerous threat to our ultimate aims, no discussion, let alone serious consideration, was permitted during the war on how to meet this threat.

When the Allied armies were advancing across Europe, all decisions on the speed and extent of the advance to meet the oncoming Red Army were left largely to the generals in the field. As a result, Berlin, Prague and large sections of central Germany were left to the Russians to conquer with far-reaching political consequences. The responsibility must of course be shared by the American political leadership which was, at the time, overly optimistic about the future of Russian-American relations. The chief military consideration which dictated our stopping short of Berlin or Prague was, according to the generals, the cost in casualties. But as Clausewitz pointed out, the cost in effort is not a military decision at all but a purely political one and one that the political leaders should have decided.

Those who served in European commands during the war can doubtless cite dozens of minor examples of a similar nature in which the advice of the political branch, though always available, was seldom sought and even less frequently followed by American generals.

Nor was this habit confined to the European theater. In the Yalta negotiations with Stalin on Russian participation in the war against Japan, the decision was made to offer extensive territories belonging to Japan and China to the Soviet Union as an inducement to enter the war. The author of a recent scholarly study of these negotiations, Louis Morton, concludes: "The decision to seek Soviet participation provides one of the clearest examples in recent years of the subordination of the political to the military considerations of policy. No one can study these negotiations and not be struck by the almost complete absence of political representation."*

One could continue to cite instances of similar decisions in the Korean War and even in military operations since then but the illustrations above should, I think, be sufficient to make the point clear. In view of the damage these military-made decisions caused to our postwar political posture, they should also provide proof of the wisdom of Clausewitz' proposition.

But it should also be emphasized that this tendency to subordinate political to military considerations in wartime is not usually the fault of overambitious generals. Indeed, in many cases the need for them to make decisions is thrust upon them by the default of the highest political authorities and only accepted with great reluctance.

The implications for unconventional warfare of the predominance of the political over the military point of view is obvious. It will not have escaped the reader's notice that practically all the crucial problems of the guerrilla and the counterguerrilla operations discussed in previous chapters are political. The military stratagems and tactics are secondary means to an end.

This relationship has been clearly recognized by the Communist practitioners of the art. "It is vital that simple-minded militarists be made to realize the relationship that exists between politics and military affairs," Mao Tse-tung wrote bluntly, paraphrasing Clausewitz, whom he had studied. He also wrote: "Military action is a method used to attain a political goal. While military affairs and political affairs are not identical, it is impossible to isolate one from the other." In his study of irregular warfare, Mao Tse-tung devotes at least as much space to a discussion

* "Soviet Intervention in the War with Japan," *Foreign Affairs*, July 1962, Vol. 40, No. 4, p. 662.

of the political implications of the role of the irregular as to his purely military functions. "Political activities," he maintains, "are the life of both the guerrilla armies and revolutionary warfare."

Stalin, by divorcing the Partisan movement from the military apparatus of the Soviet High Command and by subordinating it completely to the political machine within the Communist Party, likewise emphasized the political priorities of unconventional warfare.

We have already called attention to the predominance of political over military training among other successful guerrilla leaders; among them Ho Chi Minh, Giap and Tito.

Magsaysay, the anti-Communist counterinsurgent, similarly recognized the primacy of political over military measures. While he made vigorous use of his troops to contain the guerrillas and protect the population from them, the cures he applied were mainly political.

During the early stages of the Communist uprising in Greece, when the British were supporting the counterinsurgents, they discovered that in directing the efforts of the anti-Communist forces a handful of classical scholars, who in their researches had roamed the Greek countryside for years, were at least as effective as a whole company of troops specially trained in the techniques of guerrilla operations.

American experience in guerrilla warfare goes back to pre-Revolutionary days when the colonists were engaged in a continuous unconventional war with the Indians. When the Revolution broke out, one of the veterans of these wars, Francis Marion, a farmer by trade, became a guerrilla raider in the classical sense of the word and was nicknamed "the Swamp Fox" by the British General Cornwallis. Cornwallis, reflecting the professional view toward guerrillas prevalent among British and other soldiers, also charged that he fought neither "like a gentleman" nor "a Christian."

During the Civil War a Southern lawyer, John Mosby, gained

fame for his exploits behind the Northern lines. His reputation for long-distance rapid strikes caused such a panic in Washington at one time that the planks on the Chain Bridge over the Potomac were removed every night lest Mosby stage a raid and take the President himself prisoner.

And, of course, during a good part of the nineteenth century, American troops were engaged in the Western territories in guerrilla warfare against Indian bands.

The Philippine insurrection at the turn of the century provided another opportunity for irregular warfare. But in all of these cases, it will be noted the irregulars operated either as auxiliaries to regular armies or as counterinsurgent forces.

However, it was not until World War II that American forces came into contact with modern, sophisticated guerrilla movements. In the jungles of Southeast Asia, Americans helped organize and lead guerrilla bands against the Japanese. In France and Italy, American parachutists provided aid and maintained liaison with resistance groups against the German occupation. In Yugoslavia, American teams participated in numerous sabotage undertakings with Tito's Partisans and maintained liaison staffs both with Tito and Mikhailovitch.

A few of these missions were manned by professional officers but the great majority were recruited from civilians by the Office of Strategic Services. Few if any had had any experience whatever with modern guerrilla operations. Their training consisted largely in the techniques of parachuting, sabotage and demolition, communications and supply drops, guerrilla tactics, weaponry and occasionally a lecture or two on the political background of the areas to which they were to be assigned.

The technical training was relatively simple and easily accomplished. The political training was less successful for the obvious reason that years, not months, were necessary to acquire an adequate knowledge of the political and social terrain. And years were not available. Language training, too, was a very important and difficult problem since only a knowledge of local languages could provide the liaison observer with independent access to local opinion. To a certain extent this deficiency, as we have noted, was overcome by enlisting first- and second-generation *émigrés* from the areas but, as we have also pointed out, the prejudices of these individuals occasionally adversely affected their objectivity.

Largely as a result of these inadequacies, the essential information on which to base policy decisions regarding our attitude toward guerrilla movements was often lacking or downright misleading. Communist leaders were often described as liberal nationalists or agrarian reformers and genuine democratic movements as "Fascist."

Nevertheless, by the time the war was over, a good start had been made in developing a nucleus of trained and experienced officers. At that time serious effort was made to persuade the authorities in the Pentagon that this nucleus be retained in government service where their dearly acquired skills would be available in the event of further "liberation war" efforts by the Communists.

These recommendations were to no avail on the ostensible ground that such "élite" groups were incompatible with the American democratic tradition. However, mistaking method for substance, a nucleus of psychological warfare experts were retained, largely as a result of the newly acquired respectability of this technique in the course of World War II.

Not until the Kremlin called its agents in Southeast Asia to arms three years later did it gradually become apparent that to combat Communist movements something more than conventional troops and propaganda specialists was required. Consequently a Special Forces school was established, and several battalions of troops trained in guerrilla tactics were organized.

Later these were expanded until today more than 10,000 troops have been trained in unconventional warfare techniques and have acquired a smattering of political instruction, including the languages of some of the areas threatened by Communist guerrilla tactics.

These efforts, tardy though they were, were not only valuable but indeed, as things have turned out, essential. The Special Forces schools at Fort Bragg and elsewhere are staffed with highly competent, intelligent and imaginative officers who are, to the best of their opportunities and facilities, training key cadres in the elements of guerrilla tactics and counterinsurgency. The Special Forces, in turn, have proved invaluable in helping stem the tide of Communist subversion in Vietnam.

The only defect of these measures is that they overlook the principle problem of providing political direction for the counterinsurgent forces. The cases studied in previous chapters demonstrate that guerrilla war is a continuation of political intercourse chiefly by political means and supplemented by military, economic, sociological and psychological measures. Hence it would be as absurd to put such operations under purely military direction as it would be to ask a radio engineer to produce a television program. While the technician is essential as an auxiliary, without suitable direction any success he may have as a producer is purely fortuitous.

Clausewitz warned as we have noted that the political element should not "sink deep into the details" of conventional war. Nor is it suggested here that the political element should "sink deep" into the technical details of unconventional war any more than a general in Vietnam would snatch the controls of a helicopter from the hands of its pilot.

However, in contrast to conventional war, the political problems of unconventional war lie largely in day-to-day operations in the field. The choice between civic action and military action, between reprisal and persuasion, reform or repression in any given situation; between napalm and pamphlets; between which villages to uproot and which to defend; between which areas to attack and which to befriend—all these are basically political decisions which must be made in the field and on the spot—not by directives from home. When in the past they have been decided by wise political leadership in the field they have generally been successful. Magsaysay, the politician, defeated the Huks where the generals had failed. Mao, the librarian, defeated Chiang Kai-shek, the professional warlord. The history teacher, Giap, not the French Marshal, Navarre, won at Dien Bien Phu. Tito, the Communist political agent, not Mikhailovitch, the monarchist professional soldier, won in Yugoslavia.

Some, no doubt, will regard the idea of subordinating the military in the field to political directors ("political commissars"?) as a novel, radical and distasteful innovation. So too did the tradition-steeped marshals of Austria and Prussia with their precious, precision-trained little armies regard that earlier innovation, the citizens' army of France. But their disdain helped them little as Napoleon's rabble swept them to defeat.

Of that earlier innovation in warfare, the Prussian professional Clausewitz wrote: "The prodigious effect of the French Revolution abroad was brought about much less through new methods and views introduced by the French in the conduct of war than through the changes it wrought in statecraft and civil administration, in the character of governments, in the conditions of people, etc. That other governments took a mistaken view of all these things; that they endeavored, with their ordinary means, to hold their own against forces of a novel kind and overwhelming in strength—all that was a blunder in policy."

The challenge posed by modern unconventional warfare and particularly by "liberation wars" is not one of new methods. Guerrillas are as old as Sung Tzu. The challenge is that made possible by the replacement of colonial administrations with popular governments and by the aspirations of new nations exploited by Communist political subversion. In meeting this modern and novel challenge we can, like the adversaries of Napoleon, blunder along with "ordinary means" or we can adopt modern concepts and new procedures for the effective employment of our available forces.

In proposing political direction of the military in unconventional war, I do not mean to suggest in any way that the political branch of the government has a monopoly of political acumen or that the military in the Pentagon has a monopoly of political myopia. Several of the most astute political minds of our generation have been in uniform and today many officers in all three branches of the service undoubtedly have the intelligence, political vision and enthusiasm to make excellent political directors of an American unconventional force.

However, unless an officer is prepared to forget much of what he has been taught throughout his training about conventional warfare and to forgo his future military career, it is doubtful whether he can develop the skills and values he will need to become a professional in the political problems of guerrilla operations. From the personal point of view alone, to ask a regular officer to spend several years of his career in an activity so remote from his primary profession is not only unfair to him but unproductive. In guerrilla war, the subjects that a professional soldier has devoted himself to during all his career become only a minor ingredient in the complete mixture—and in a form quite different from that which he studied on the sand-tables of his military schools.

The main ingredient, a knowledge of the political and social terrain of the area to which he may be assigned, requires an entirely different curriculum of training and experience.

The same criticism may be made of the practice of training in our Special Forces schools the military personnel of friendly countries that may be threatened by subversive war. Defending this practice, it has been suggested that in countries with weak governments the military are generally the most stabilizing influence. But they are by the same token generally representatives of the most conservative element least disposed to adopt the moderate counterinsurgent methods of Magsaysay and most inclined to meet rebellion with the questionable weapons of repression and reprisal.

Once again may I reiterate that these comments are in no sense meant as a disparagement of the competence of our military leaders. As an ex-cavalry officer, I often think that the senior generals of the Pentagon are like high-mettled, well-schooled, courageous officers' chargers on whom a heedless, irresponsible public led by Congress has piled burden after burden until with tendons taut and nostrils distended, they stagger precariously through the slippery streets of Washington. Educated at West Point to fight the battles of World War I, they have suddenly found themselves saddled with managing the greatest industrial enterprise in history, directing the most advanced scientific laboratories the world has seen, and now, finally, assigned to command the most intricate and sophisticated political operations of our generation. Publicly they assume a bold, unflinching front but in private those of them who understand the magnitude of their tasks plead to be divested of their intolerable burdens. "We are doing the best we can," they say, "but the job is beyond us."

If the military is unsuited to direct unconventional warfare and counterinsurgent operations, what civilian agency of the government is qualified? The State Department's Foreign Service is by training and experience in some ways more adequately equipped. However, as the Communists have discovered, formal diplomacy and unconventional operations are basically incompatible and should, if only on security grounds, be kept strictly apart. Further-more, the cosmopolitan atmosphere of diplomatic life is hardly likely to develop those characteristics needed for the more rugged and earthy aspects of unconventional warfare.

The Bay of Pigs operation was directed by the Central Intelligence Agency, though in the basic decisions it seems to have deferred to the military. But the fundamental conflict between intelligence gathering and policy making imposes a severe handicap on the CIA's activities in unconventional warfare operations.

The dilemma is not unrecognized by those responsible in high places of government. Military officials charged with unconventional warfare readily admit the inadequacy of their training and of the political background available to them for the task. Highly placed civilian officials recognize that the political element in unconventional warfare is of vital importance, though they tend to veil their intellectual conclusions in earthier admonitions about the necessity of killing guerrillas too. The National Security Council, which brings together political and military advice, would seem to recognize, at least in part, the essentially political character of all military undertakings.

The conflict of aims and interest between American political, military and intelligence agencies overseas has long been apparent. To mitigate this conflict the "country-team" method has been devised whereby a committee representing the various services, political and military, has been formed in American embassies under the chairmanship of the ambassadors, who are technically at least the personal representatives of the President and as such the senior American officials in the countries to which they are accredited.

However, this technical seniority has not always been recognized, especially by military personnel, who for generations have considered themselves under the direct orders of their superiors in Washington and not subordinated in purely military matters to mere civilians whatever their technical or diplomatic rank. While they are more or less forced reluctantly to "consult and keep [the Ambassador] informed," as their orders read, they do not always recognize his command authority. To correct this misconception, each of the last three Presidents, including President Kennedy, has issued what would seem to be unequivocal directives stating that the ambassador is indeed the senior American representative. However, even these directives have failed to overcome the deep-seated concept that in military matters military men are supreme. For example, in Vietnam, though the ambassador is acknowledged to be in over-all charge of the American support effort, the most cursory reading of the daily newspapers leaves the distinct impression that the senior general and not the ambassador is in command. When the decision to re-enforce the American effort in Vietnam was made in 1961, for instance, it was the military contingent in Saigon, not the political, which was augmented by a covey of new generals.

Under the Kennedy administration, however, a more practical and effective step to eliminate the conflicts between the political and military services has been taken by the formation of the "Special Group, C.I." (counter-insurgency) in Washington. As the Washington counterpart of the country teams, this group is in a sense the pinnacle of the country-team structure. Under the chairmanship of Under Secretary of State Averell Harriman, Special Group is formed of representatives of the principle government agencies with overseas interests including, besides the State Department, the Defense Department, Central Intelligence and others. Among its members are some of the most dynamic and able political leaders in the government including the President's brother Robert, one of its most enthusiastic and active participants.

Though it has no permanent staff and no institutional role in the government's structure, Special Group has been most effective not merely in settling disputes in the country teams but, more important, as their representative in Washington, expediting measures for their support, e.g., the obtaining of special equipment they may need or of funds for civic action operations. Still more important, it has guided the teams by defining their aims and by initiating many measures to spur counter-insurgency operations overseas, to forestall situations where insurgency threatens and, one hopes, to plan for insurgency operations where they may be needed in future. Thus, for example, the Group has been instrumental in setting up a training school in the Panama Canal Zone for police forces of countries where incipient guerrilla movements if not dealt with in time might threaten friendly governments.

Since the majority of its members are civilian, political figures, the Special Group as presently constituted effectively assures that political aims remain dominant over temporary or purely military objectives.

However, it does so despite rather than because of popularly accepted American doctrine. Furthermore it has many of the earmarks and disadvantages of other *ad hoc* solutions. As an informal group meeting once a week, it owes its effectiveness largely if not exclusively to the dynamic personalities and prestige of its individual members. With no permanent constitutional existence, it is at the mercy of whatever influences are currently dominant in Washington. Thus with a change of administration it might well disappear without a ripple from the scene, leaving the old concepts to guide the formulation of policy. Even more likely, if less energetic and able persons were to replace its present members it would in all probability join the long rank of other *ad hoc* committees which like ghosts haunt the government's corridors and payrolls.

Reluctantly one is forced to the conclusion that the problem remains unsolved and that the basic public misconception of the relationship of politics to war that has guided American policies in the past has not been permanently disposed of.

However, once it is popularly recognized that a military effort by the United States is not a moral crusade to destroy the forces of some foreign devil but a means to a political end, and that guerrilla warfare in particular is a highly sophisticated political operation, it should not be difficult to fit a permanent command post for its direction into the national administrative structure.

The Irregular Warfare Command need not be a large one. It would suffice, it seems to me, to maintain a small staff with a few specialists carefully selected for their sound political judgment and practical flair for irregular operations, each of whom would be assigned to a specific potentially dangerous area and be ready, if necessary, to lead an American counterinsurgent operation or to advise an Allied operation. This staff would be recruited from all available sources: Foreign Service, military and CIA personnel and from civilians, particularly from ethnic groups originating from the potential trouble spots and who have the special linguistic and local knowledge, but avoiding recent *émigrés* still dominated by local loyalties and prejudices. The staff should, of course, be on permanent assignment with career prerogatives like those of the other services.

Among their responsibilities would be the instruction of the army's and other services' Special Forces in the political aspects of irregular warfare and they should maintain the closest personal contact with the officers commanding these units who, in times of actual operations, would be subordinated to them as military auxiliaries and technicians. They should themselves attend the Special Forces schools and become proficient in the technical skills they teach such as parachuting, demolition and communications. Similarly, they should maintain close contact with the United States Information Agency from which in time of need they would recruit personnel as propaganda auxiliaries.

Above all, they should concern themselves not only with the theory of irregular warfare but with the practical problems likely to be encountered in the areas of their responsibility. Of paramount importance would be their knowledge of the terrain of those areas, the political personalities in the government and in the opposition, the issues likely to be exploited by instigators of "liberation wars," the prejudices and taboos, the aspirations and grievances of all elements of the population and, of course, their languages and dialects. For this purpose they should be given the widest opportunity and suitable cover to travel and live among the people with whom one day they may be operating as comrades-in-arms or as enemies.

Ideally, it seems to me, the staff should be directly subordinated to the National Security Council for long-range and operational directives. For its day-to-day guidance it should rely on the State Department. For security reasons it should probably receive its logistic and household support through the Central Intelligence Agency, though like other divisions of the Agency in the past, it should be carefully separated from its intelligence gathering and analysis functions.

The precise details of its organizational position and structure are not as crucial as the principle that the staff would exercise the over-all political command and leadership essential to an effective irregular warfare operation. Until this principle is put into practice, I fear that a key element of our national power potential will continue to wallow in Bays of Pigs.

Index

ABOUT THE AUTHOR

Charles W. Thayer was born in Villanova, Pennsylvania, in 1910. Educated at St. Paul's School and West Point, he resigned his commission as Second Lieutenant in the Cavalry shortly after graduation, and was appointed to the career Foreign Service in 1937. He served in Russia, Germany, Afghanistan, and Persia; then in London on the European Advisory Commission, planning the occupation of Germany with the British and Russians.

In 1943, Mr. Thayer received a military leave from the Foreign Service, and, after attending parachute school in England, was assigned as Chief of the U.S. Military Mission to Marshal Tito in Yugoslavia. There he served with Tito's Partisans and gained a first-hand knowledge of guerrilla warfare. Subsequently, he was involved in intelligence operations as head of the OSS Mission in Austria, and acted as interpreter and advisor on Russian affairs to the U.S. High Commander, General Mark Clark.

In 1946, Mr. Thayer was named Political Commissioner on the U.S.-U.S.S.R. Commission for Korea and served six months in Seoul negotiating for the unification of that country. After attending the National War College in Washington, D.C., he started the first broadcasts to the Soviet Union on the Voice of America, and was head of the Voice of America from 1947 to 1949.

Mr. Thayer was then sent back to duty in Germany, where he was assigned as Political Liaison Officer to the newly formed Federal Republic in Bonn. He played a part in drafting Adenauer's proposal to contribute twelve German divisions to NATO. In 1952, he transferred to Munich as Consul General and Land Commissioner for Bavaria.

While in the Foreign Service Mr. Thayer published his first two books, *Bears in the Caviar* and *Hands Across the Caviar,* humorous reminiscences of his diplomatic life. In 1953, he resigned from the Foreign Service and has since devoted himself entirely to writing. Mr. Thayer and his wife now divide their time between their homes in Washington and Germany and traveling, primarily in Iron Curtain countries.

Format by Sidney Feinberg
Set in Linotype Times Roman
Composed, printed and bound by The Haddon Craftsmen, Inc.
HARPER & ROW, PUBLISHERS

DATE DUE

MAR 11 '69			
MAR 26 69			
FEB 25 '70			
OCT 1 8 1981			